Freedom's Journey

Jacob Hiebert

TEACH Services, Inc.
P U B L I S H I N G
www.TEACHServices.com • (800) 367-1844

Copyright © 2021 Jacob Hiebert

Copyright © 2021 TEACH Services, Inc.

ISBN-13: 978-1-4796-1274-1 (Paperback)

ISBN-13: 978-1-4796-1275-8 (ePub)

Library of Congress Control Number: 2020919812

All Scripture quotations are taken from the King James Version® of the Bible. Public domain.

TEACH Services, Inc.
P U B L I S H I N G
www.TEACHServices.com • (800) 367-1844

Dedication

I want to dedicate this book to my parents, David and Helene Hiebert, whose Christian life of practice and example impressed upon me the importance of the Bible teachings as supreme and above that of man's devising's or church creeds.

To Judy, my dear wife and love of my life, who has been a strong encouragement to me to record how God brought our family safely through the most discouraging times of life when we put our trust in Him. Judy stood by my side to assist me with her computer expertise, secretarial skills, and help with the style and structure of this manuscript in preparation for printing.

I would also like to make special mention of my longtime friend, Dr. Barry Bussey, who envisioned the blessings of putting in print our experiences of how God brought us through some very trying times when the world conditions were most discouraging.

I am also indebted to Carolyn Willis, a dear friend of our family from the years of our service in Ontario. Carolyn has been a tremendous blessing with her editorial and structural skills.

Table of Contents

Foreword **By Dr. Barry Bussey** 7

Chapter 1 The Beginning of a Journey 10

Chapter 2 Rest in a Restless World 19

Chapter 3 A Day to Remember 33

Chapter 4 Years Without Dad 47

Chapter 5 Protection in Crisis 59

Chapter 6 Family Reunion 69

Chapter 7 Crossing the Swamp 81

Chapter 8 Escape to Freedom 88

Chapter 9 In Search of Liberty 98

Chapter 10 Continual Guidance and Care 109

Bibliography 121

Foreword

My first meeting of Pastor Jacob Hiebert was when I was a high school boarding student at Kingsway College, in Oshawa, Ontario. That was in the early 1980s. Little did I know that we would live in close proximity many years later in Newfoundland and later were colleagues in Ontario. As colleagues we became great friends enjoying many hours of fellowship.

I will never forget, for two reasons, the time in Newfoundland, 1993, when Jacob and Judy invited my family over for a Sabbath meal after church. First reason, my children, Carmelle age four, Adam and Seth age two thoroughly enjoyed the scrumptious meal that Judy served, so much so that they made audible guttural "mmmhmmm!" as they had desert. We had a great laugh over that.

Second, it was after our meal that Jacob told us but a wee bit of his childhood deliverance from the ravages of war-torn Europe. By nature, Jacob is a natural storyteller. He has his audience spellbound as he develops the word pictures that literally take the hearer right into the story itself so that you are as if a third person watching the story unfold in real time. I have met only a few people in my lifetime that has that ability—and Jacob is one of them—as you will soon find out.

I listened intently to the story of his family's crossing the border from East Germany to West Germany. I never heard anything like it before. I could only imagine what people, without freedom, had to suffer. Of course, I watched many WWII movies over the years that try to convey what that experience was like, but when you hear it directly from a survivor you are taken to a different level altogether. I wanted more.

A few years later I served as in-house legal counsel for the Ontario Conference of the Seventh-day Adventist Church and as part of my responsibilities I worked in the area of Public Affairs and Religious Liberty (PARL). Seventh-day Adventists promote religious freedom for everyone. I learned to appreciate those willing to stand for conscience. It occurred to me that at the Ottawa religious freedom rally I organized that Jacob's story would be a great draw for the people. I and the people of Ottawa were not disappointed with Jacob's retelling of his family's stories. Those stories—such as his father's keeping the Sabbath in communist Ukraine while working for a communist official—made an indelible imprint on my mind.

I longed for the day to see Jacob's stories in print and mentioned it to him occasionally. I am sure it got laborious for him over time to hear me ask, "So, how is the writing going?" He would chuckle and say he hoped to do it one day. My father's words came to mind when as a child he said, "By and by." I learned that things that were to happen "by and by" rarely happened. I feared that the busyness of life would crowd out Jacob's opportunity to write his story.

What joy then was mine when he sent me an e-mail that his book was finished! As soon as I opened his e-mail, I called him right away. This was a cause for celebration! Jacob's story would be told to the world—forever enshrined in a book that many can hear of God's leadership in one family's experience during WWII and shortly thereafter. A story of intense struggle for freedom that led to Canada! As Jacob recounts his arrival in Canada, "[O]ur long journey had finally come to an end. Oh, the price of freedom! Do we really always value it as we should?"

That is a sobering question.

It is always the case that we forget just how good we have things until they are removed. As I write this note, the world is going through the COVID-19 crisis. Locked up in our homes for days on end, we suddenly realize just how good it was only a few weeks before when there was no fear of catching the dreaded virus!

This book in your hand is another reminder of just how precious freedom—religious freedom, freedom to live your life without fear of the state—really is. Jacob's story is a story of people coming to understand what is important in life. As their friend Lena found out when she cast off her wheelbarrow of life's few treasures on the side of the road because she could no longer push it. "I will be free from this burden," she said. "Whatever we need, God will again supply."

Jacob understood that "war was hell." He saw how the untold suffering caused many to lose their faith and such former believers "were the first ones to report those who still tried to gather together for worship services."

Communism and war. Hunger and thirst. Fear and stress. Leaving it all behind and fleeing for freedom is something that any young child could not forget. He pleaded with his mother, Helene, "When will God give us a house again?" He walked kilometre after kilometre with other refugees on the dusty roads not knowing where the next meal was coming from. His father, David, taken forcibly from the family. Fear of what soldiers would do to his teenage sister, Erna. And, the worry of family members who were never heard of again.

Along the way people fell by the wayside and as Jacob tells us, "The dead were merely wrapped in a blanket, if one was available, and placed in a hastily dug grave that the next of kin or friends had quickly prepared. They were buried and left behind with no time to mourn their loss, or mark their last resting place."

Despite it all Jacob's family held on to their faith. "Some believed that it was impossible to survive the terror of these times, but our Heavenly Father did not forget His children who put their abiding trust in Him. It was during these most difficult years that our experience with our God reached an all-time high, never to be erased from our memories."

This is a story of faith and true grit that we will not forget. Nor should we.

—Barry W. Bussey, PhD

Chapter 1

The Beginning of a Journey

It was another bright day so common in this beautiful area of the world where I now dwell. Refreshed after a morning's walk and feeling inspired by nature's sounds of chickadees and robins, of chattering squirrels and flower beds tumbling their colorful blossoms over the edges of tidy borders as if not able to contain the gladness of the season, I knew it was time, time to put on paper the thoughts that had been evolving in my mind for many months, ready to emerge in written form.

One of the most important lessons I have learned while traveling this journey called life is just how precious this life is. I also recognize that the true purpose and meaning of life is often lost sight of in the myriad of activities and interruptions that are thrust upon us every waking hour. The busyness that we allow to intrude into our days causes us not to recognize and appreciate its true value.

I have also learned through the years that God's purpose and goal for our life, both now and throughout eternity, is far beyond the finite mind's greatest imagination. One of my favorite authors beautifully penned this thought when she wrote, "Higher than the highest human thought can reach is God's ideal for His children."[1]

So, where does it all begin and end? It begins with our Creator, the God of the universe. God said of Jeremiah, *"Before I formed thee in the*

---

1   Ellen G. White, Education (Mountain View, CA: Pacific Press, 1903), p. 18.

belly I knew thee; and before thou camest forth out of the womb I sanctified thee" (Jer. 1:5). What love and care God lavishes on His children. Before I was even born God knew all about me and He had a perfect plan for my life. It is His greatest desire that I will choose to accept His plan so that I might live a more abundant life, not only now, but throughout eternity. I am aware that all I have experienced through the various trying circumstances in past years has helped me to see God's plan for my life more clearly.

This is the story of that life. As you read, perhaps you too will recognize God's leading in the sometimes eager and sometimes faltering footsteps of my journey.

I have often been asked, "What is your nationality?" The answer to this question is not as easy as it would appear. My ancestors were from Holland, yet I am German. I spent many years in Germany. I went to school there and can read and write the language fluently. German is the language of my birth, yet I was born in Ukraine. For the past seventy years Canada has been my home, arriving to this country in 1949. All but four years of my education in public schools, high school, college and universities has been in Canada and the United States. I have mastered the English language and I am proud to be a Canadian citizen.

Many parts of the world have shaped my life and brought me to where I am today, but Canada has given me and my family the freedom that I value more than tongue can express. I will always be grateful for the privilege of living where I can worship my Creator without fearing persecution as it now exists in many countries of the world.

Now let me share with you how life has brought me to where I am today. It has been a long and marvelous journey through countries where freedom of any kind was not to be found.

My life began with the beginning of World War II, however, there was much that transpired hundreds of years before that would influence my thinking and outlook on life. It would especially influence my relationship with God and my religious commitment thereafter.

During the fifteenth century, there was a great religious movement throughout Europe. Its influence spread to most of the countries of the world, and in a large degree to North America, a Protestant nation at its birth. This was a time known as the Protestant Reformation. During this time my ancestors in Holland were Roman Catholic.

Martin Luther (1483–1546) of Germany, a Catholic priest and university professor, was an ardent student of the Bible. He set about to introduce major reforms within the Catholic Church. It was not his intent to leave the established church of his day, but he believed that the Bible was of supreme authority and its teaching was above the authority of the church. He was also convinced from a study of the Bible that man was saved through faith and not works. Luther's teachings did not find favor with the established church and, as a result, it dealt severely with him. Standing before the Diet of Worms, he was required to renounce his convictions, but instead spoke those words that have been repeated down through the ages, "I cannot and I will not retract, for it is unsafe for a Christian to speak against his conscience. Here I stand, I can do no other; may God help me. Amen."[2] A death sentence was declared against him, but due to God's direct intervention, his friends came to his aid and saved his life. As a result of his work, the Protestant Reformation gained great strength in Europe.

Martin Luther was one of the main leaders of the Protestant Reformation in Europe, but there were many others prior, during and after Luther who had a part in this reformation. Men such as John Wycliffe of England in the fourteenth century, Hus and Jerome of Bohemia, Ulrich Zwingli of Switzerland, Lefevre of France, Tyndale and John Wesley of England, all of whom vowed to remain faithful to the gospel that brought them such joy and comfort, even as their lives were being threatened. All of these Reformers had one thing in common in that they took the Bible as their only rule of faith.

My forefathers in Holland witnessed the teachings of Menno Simons (1496–1564), a Dutch religious reformer and leader in Holland and Germany. They came to accept the teachings of the Bible as presented by Menno Simons, who at first was of the Anabaptists. His adherents were known as Mennonites after the name of their leader. Shortly thereafter they experienced a great persecution from the Catholic Church, which had heretofore been the state church of most of the countries of Europe. The religious persecution increased to such an extent that it was impossible to worship according to the dictates of ones' conscience.

As my forefathers, who were now of the Mennonite faith, looked for a place that would allow them the religious freedom they so desired, they turned their eyes towards northern Germany. This was Luther's country and due to his work there, most of northern Germany were followers of the Lutheran faith. Religious freedom was granted to those of other faiths as well who chose to follow the Bible rather than the authority of the

---

2   Ellen G. White, The Great Controversy (Mountain View, CA: Pacific Press, 1911), p. 160.

established church. The decision was made to escape the religious persecution in that part of Holland and make the move to northern Germany.

This was not an easy decision for them as they were forced to make
major life adjustments. It was a new country with a new language to learn,
and a different government, but in spite of the difficulties they relished
in the freedom of this new environment. Here they decided to establish
new homes and put behind them the years of persecution they had experienced in their homeland. After a lengthy time in northern Germany, my
ancestors were faced with another decision to pull up stakes and move on.

Catherine the Great (1729–1796) of Russia, a German-born empress
who was a strong ruler in Russia, was looking for people who were well
experienced in agriculture, and who were willing to come to the Ukraine
to settle as pioneers in the southern part of the country.

As the Mennonite people were well known for their expertise in
farming the land productively, she put forth a special offer to those that
were willing to relocate. She offered free homesteading to the Mennonite
farmers. As a result of this attractive offer, there was a great exodus to
southern Ukraine. My forefathers were among those who ventured out
to establish new farming communities in a new land. This was well before
the time of communism in Russia, and what would later be known as the
Soviet Union. All Mennonite settlers were granted religious freedom and
were not required to bear arms in the event of a war.

The land was very productive and became known as the "breadbasket
of Russia." Approximately thirty villages or towns soon sprang up result-
ing in a thriving economy. All the persecutions of the past were soon put
behind them. They worked hard and were blessed with a prosperity they
had not experienced for many years.

My grandfather, David Hiebert, made a good living, having acquired
three farms when he was still in his early forties. He was also a cabinet
maker. As a cabinet maker he was called upon to make caskets, a task he
soon developed a distaste for as during this particular time in history, due
to wars, famine, plagues and uprisings, many untimely deaths occurred.
As a respected member of his community, my great grandfather, who was
also named David Hiebert was elected as mayor of one of the towns where
most of my ancestors had settled. For about five generations in my family
the oldest son was always called David, which makes it hard to keep track
of the right generation.

My grandfather David and his wife Agatha were blessed with three
children. The eldest, David, my father, was born in 1896, followed by a
daughter, Agatha, named after her mother, born in 1904 and Katherina in

1908. His plan was to turn over the farming business to his son as well as provide for his daughters.

(left to right) My dad, one year old, Grandma Agatha and Grandpa David Hiebert in 1897

The future looked bright, and when my father showed an interest in furthering his education, Grandfather discouraged him from doing so, stating that the farming operation would more than meet any future financial needs. However, Dad felt that a little more education could not hurt. His slogan was, "Whatever you have in your head, no one can take from you." During these early years (1914), finishing the eleventh year of school was almost the equivalent of having a college degree today. It wasn't long before he would experience the wisdom of his decision. His eleventh-grade education in the earliest years of the nineteenth century proved to be a tremendous blessing to him throughout his life in many countries of Europe as he was able to serve as pastor and teacher.

My dad was a born leader, good in organizing his work in a productive manner and taking charge of very difficult projects and situations. It was this gift, with God's blessing, that would later help us escape from the clutches of communism during the years of World War II, when thousands were sent to concentration camps or to Siberia, never to be heard from again.

Dad (bottom right) with soldiers of WWI as noncombatant "Cook"

The year was 1917 when the unthinkable happened—a situation the world could never have foreseen or been prepared for. The tsarist regime was overthrown in Russia, and Vladimir Ilyich Lenin (1870–1924) came to power. With him, communism was promoted in Russia as well as the countries that were under its jurisdiction, commonly known as the USSR, which included Ukraine. This brought about a complete dissolution of law and order in the Russian Empire. The envy of those less willing to work and, therefore, the poorer population now could get without punishment what the state laws before had forbidden—the rich properties of the Mennonites. Murder, robberies, plunder and terrorization by kidnapping and intimidation were the order of the day. The state was unable to protect the settlers and they were unable to defend themselves because of their faith. Within a short time, the situation became impossible and most of the settlers were forced to flee from their villages without their possessions. As communism gained strength, the government took possession of all properties. All the land now became the property of the government, and the former landowners became tenants required to work the land giving its major yield to the government, now the legal owner of all lands. Life had taken an abrupt turn for the settlers who had envisioned living out their lives in this peaceful, pastoral region of the Ukraine.

My grandfather, who had been well set financially with his three farms, now lost everything he had worked for. The loss of his livelihood, provision for his children after him, along with major changes in the laws of the country as a whole brought about by the communist regime, took a heavy toll on his health. In 1919, at the early age of forty-five, he passed to his rest leaving a young family behind.

No longer was there religious freedom. Since atheism is the practiced religion of communism, there was no God as far as the Communist Party was concerned. Most churches were either turned into museums, or in rural areas, they were used as granaries to store crops that were harvested from the land. People were encouraged to join the Communist Party, but many, including Grandfather's family, could not conscientiously do this, and therefore were considered second-rate citizens.

Unannounced, the secret police would make periodic checks on everyone, and if they were not pleased with what they found, arrests were made, punishment was administered and, in many cases, people were sent to concentration camps or Siberia. Many relatives of my parents' immediate family were sent to Siberia, living under the most extreme of winter conditions. My parents were able to keep in contact with some of them for a time and others, like my mother's oldest brother, were never heard from again. Living conditions became increasingly worse as time went on. The people were stripped of any feelings of security for themselves and their families. Even the children were forcibly educated by the state to ensure their allegiance to the state rather than to their own parents. They were required to report any actions that did not show obedience to the state and communism.

Father decided that he and his family could no longer live under these conditions. Something must be done, but whatever it was, must be planned with the greatest secrecy so as not to arouse suspicion with the authorities. For a time, the borders were still open and people with special permission could immigrate to other countries provided that they were in good health. They also needed government approval which was not always easily acquired.

After the necessary arrangements were finalized, health certificates acquired and government permission obtained, my grandmother Agatha Hiebert, and her daughter, Agatha, filled with a mixture of relief and sadness, immigrated to Ontario, Canada. The year was 1925 and shortly thereafter the border closed and no one was allowed to leave the country.

(left to right) Aunt Agatha Hiebert,
Grandma Agatha Hiebert

You may wonder why my dad and his youngest sister, Katherina, did not join my grandmother and also move to Canada, a land of freedom. Actually, that was indeed the plan. However, my dad and mother were married in June 29, 1924, the year before my grandmother and aunt left for Canada. Also, Katherina had contracted TB and so could not receive health clearance for immigration. It was with heavy hearts that my parents bid farewell to their loved ones but continued to pray that the Lord would somehow open the way for them to soon follow. Little did they then realize that they would be forced to remain in the Soviet Union until the end of World War II. The conditions in the Soviet Union became increasingly worse as time went on, but our family did not give up hope and God always came through for us even when it seemed that we were at an impasse.

Chapter 2

Rest in a Restless World

After my dad's mother and oldest sister left Ukraine en route to Canada, his youngest sister, Katherina, came under Dad's care until she married. My dad, David, had recently married my mother, Helene Schulz, a petite girl from a very religious Mennonite family and my Aunt Katherina (Dad's sister), was introduced to Mother's family. A special relationship soon developed between Mother's youngest brother, David Schulz, and Katherina. This relationship resulted in a marriage which was quite unique. Brother and sister on Dad's side married brother and sister on my mother's side.

My parents David and Helene Hiebert on their wedding day, June 29, 1924

My parents still kept in touch with Dad's mother and sister who were now in Canada as well as Canada Immigration, but they soon realized that Russia had effectively closed the border and there was little or no hope of leaving Russia any time soon—if ever.

My mother's parents now felt the effects of years of economic hardships under communism. Sickness and disease surrounded them and they were not strong enough to fight for their lives. It was a sad time for my mother when she had to say goodbye to them. It seemed that wherever one turned there was only more sorrow. After the death of my mother's parents, her youngest sister, who was still single and actually never married, came to be a part of my parent's family. In 1925, a special joy filled the home of my parents when my oldest sibling, Lydia, joined their family. These were hard times. My parents often found themselves in severe financial circumstances, often with meager provisions of food, but when it seemed as if they couldn't survive, God always came through. Dad's mother would occasionally send them food packages from Canada with some basic food items. This soon came to an end, however, when the Russians stopped all such shipments from the West. In 1927, there was renewed joy in the Hiebert home when another little girl, Erna, was born and joined the family. Our family would eventually increase to eight, two girls and four boys along with Mother and Dad. Due to poverty and various sicknesses, all but three of the children did not survive.

> *My parents often found themselves in severe financial circumstances, often with meager provisions of food, but when it seemed as if they couldn't survive, God always came through.*

(left to right) Lydia, Erna, Dad, and Mom in 1932

It was a heartbreaking blow when my oldest sister Lydia became very sick. It soon became evident that she might not recover in spite of everything that my parents tried to do to save her. Medical science was not as far advanced in those days, and due to the poor conditions and lack of nutritious food, the doctor informed my parents that he did not expect her to survive her illness. My sister was a very religious girl who understood biblical truths at a very young age. When she learned of her condition and that she would probably not get well, she was very sad. My dad, with whom she was especially close, tried to comfort her, telling her how much Jesus loved her. Then he asked her, "Are you afraid of dying?" "No," she replied, "I just wanted to live to see Jesus coming in the clouds when He comes for His people." Dad then explained to her that the Bible says that when Jesus comes, He will awaken all those who loved Him, and they will see Him coming in the clouds. The angels will then gather them and take them in the clouds to meet Jesus, and He will take them all to heaven with Him (1 Thess. 4:16–17). This news gave her so much hope that she replied with great joy, "Daddy, if I will see Jesus coming in the clouds for me and we will all be together again, I am not afraid to die." In just a few days she passed peacefully to her rest at the tender age of eight. She sleeps now in a little town in southern Ukraine, waiting for Jesus to wake her and be reunited with her family.

There would also be others in our family that would not survive those hard times. My oldest brother, David, was too weak to live beyond two weeks, and another brother was born prematurely. Only three siblings were left with their parents to fight for life under those poor conditions that communism forced upon us. Erna, the oldest of my living siblings has always been a special sister to me. During the years of war when we were refugees, she was almost like a mother to me, especially when Mother was forced to go and work on the communist farms. She is now a wonderful mother of seven children, three of whom are doctors and one who is a dentist, with the other three in other professions. She is a people person naturally drawing others to her. She was very close to our father and learned many business skills from him.

Arthur, born in 1935, was a very sick baby, but he gained strength after a couple of years and survived the hardships of war. He started school in Germany, continued his education in Canada, was educated as a teacher and later as a pastor. He is now retired, living in Texas.

And then there was me, Jacob, born in 1940 in Halbstadt, Ukraine.

House where Arthur and Jacob were born

My family once again found themselves living in a restless world. Communism saw no need of a faith in God; they were driven only by their own devised ideology. This ideology also had little or no value for human life. Unless one was a committed communist with no regard for God or fellow man, communism saw you as a threat and a person that was not a trustworthy citizen of the country.

Under these conditions, our Mennonite community supported one another as best as we could with the hope that this oppressive lifestyle would not continue forever. The Mennonite people were very industrious, living in a close community with a strong faith in God. As we would soon discover, however, they did not understand religious freedom in its truest sense when it came to one of their own that left their faith to follow another religious persuasion. If any of their members left the Mennonite faith and joined another denomination, they were regarded as infidels and were shunned by the church, by the community and sadly, by their own family. It is hard to comprehend how a people that were so severely subjected to religious persecution in Europe could forget the past and withhold this right from their own people. Of course, they did not see it as such.

It is difficult to understand this kind of philosophy. The Protestant Reformation paid a great price for religious freedom and was subject to many years of severe persecution. Thousands laid down their lives in support of the truth committed to following their religious convictions. How could this be forgotten so soon? The Protestant Reformation saw the Bible as supreme and above the authority of the established church. *Sola Scriptura* (by Scripture alone) was its slogan. Everything had to be substantiated by the Bible and the Bible alone, rather than church dogmas or creeds. Some of the greatest Reformers, including Martin Luther, urged that their followers continue searching for truth beyond the point where their leaders left them. Unfortunately, in almost every case, this was not followed. It was as if all the churches that came forth as a result of the Reformation built walls around themselves and progressed no further than their leader in the advancement of biblical truth.

For many years the established church kept the Bible away from the people and taught that only the clergy could interpret it, therefore making the word of man the authority above that of the Bible. Up to this point, however, our family had no reason to doubt our religious experience or our connection and trust in our church. The Mennonite people as a whole are very industrious and sincere, living a peaceable life with each other within their community. Our family was strong in its support of our church and its teachings and my father, a great student of the Bible, was very active in support of the church programs. His motto had always been "The Bible and the Bible alone" to support his faith. God was our only hope, and in Him we would always put our complete trust.

Now let me take you back in time in the early years when my parents first got acquainted with each other. My mother lived in a village not far from where my dad grew up. They were in their late twenties when they met, and after a time of courtship decided in 1924 to share life's joys and sorrows in a united way. Around this time, a literature evangelist by the name of Mr. Gossen visited their town selling religious books and offering to study the Bible with any that might show an interest in advancing their knowledge of the Bible. Of course, my parents, who strongly believed that one could never know too much of what the Bible taught, were eager to learn more from God's Word. They agreed to meet each week at a regular time to study in depth the major teachings of the Bible. My dad often commented in later years that those were very special times when he and Mother learned so much more about God's Word, strengthening their faith to endure the harder times which were soon to come upon them.

As the Bible studies continued and one topic after another was discussed, my parents realized that Mr. Gossen was very well versed with what the Bible taught, and everything he presented made absolute sense. When they came to the study of God's day of rest for man, he pointed out that the Sabbath was Saturday and not Sunday as they had always been taught and believed. God had never changed the day. This came as a complete shock to my parents. How could this be? They had never heard this before. Could this really be true? Was not the Sabbath only meant for the Jews? Mr. Gossen pointed out that the Sabbath was in existence long before there were any Jews. In fact, God gave it to our first parents, Adam and Eve, after they were created (*Gen. 2:2, 3*). Even Abraham, who was not a Jew, kept God's commandments hundreds of years before they were written on tables of stone and given to Moses on Mount Sinai (*Gen. 26:5*). He went on to explain that when God gave the Ten Commandments, He put the Sabbath commandment right in the middle of the ten, starting with the word "Remember" (*Exod. 20:8*). When God said "Remember," He must have known that man at one point or another might forget about the importance of the Sabbath. Even Isaiah the prophet said that on the new earth all of God's people will worship Him from one Sabbath to the next (*Isa. 66:22, 23*).

My parents were amazed to hear this. They had studied their Bible for many years. How could they have missed such an important truth? *There must be an explanation for this*, they thought. "What about Jesus? Did He keep the Sabbath, the seventh day of the week?" they asked. His answer was a positive "Yes." Jesus kept every Sabbath during His life on earth (*Luke 4:16*). He even asked His disciples to remember the Sabbath more than thirty years after His ascension (*Matt. 24:20*) during the destruction of Jerusalem in AD 70. Mr. Gossen went on to tell them that Jesus declared Himself to be Lord of the Sabbath (*Luke 6:5*) because He is the Creator of everything that exists (*John 1:1–3*), therefore, He is also the One who created the Sabbath when He created this world.

My parents were stunned at what they heard. How could this be? Mother remembered hearing many sermons from her pastor stating the importance of Sunday as God's holy day and that God wants us to keep it holy. She highly regarded her pastor and determined to ask him for all the texts in the Bible that tell us that Sunday is God's holy day of rest, and that we need to observe it as such. She would then bring her answer to the next scheduled Bible study and clear up the whole misunderstanding as she presumed it to be.

My parents then inquired, "When was the change made and how did the Christian world adopt it?" Mr. Gossen replied, "The change did not come all at once, but gradually. In the first century both Jews and Christians kept the Sabbath. In the second century, there were some problems of identification between the Jews and the early Christians. All that kept the Sabbath were labeled as Jews, therefore, some in the early Christian church worshiped on Sunday. This shift became even stronger as time went on, and by the fourth century the early Christian church had largely adopted Sunday as the day of worship." He went on to say, "The word "Sunday" does not even appear anywhere in the Bible. However, the first day of the week is mentioned eight times in the Bible, and none of those texts support the idea that it was a day of worship."

Mr. Gossen then proceeded to give them a study of these eight Bible texts:

1. *"In the end of the sabbath, as it began to dawn toward the first day of the week, came Mary Magdalene and the other Mary to see the sepulchre" (Matt. 28:1).*

2. *"And very early in the morning the first day of the week, they came unto the sepulchre at the rising of the sun" (Mark 16:2).*

3. *"Now when Jesus was risen early the first day of the week, he appeared first to Mary Magdalene, out of whom he had cast seven devils" (Mark 16:9).*

4. *"Now upon the first day of the week, very early in the morning, they came unto the sepulchre, bringing the spices which they had prepared, and certain others with them" (Luke 24:1).*

5. *"The first day of the week cometh Mary Magdalene early, when it was yet dark, unto the sepulchre, and seeth the stone taken away from the sepulchre" (John 20:1).*

6. *"Then the same day at evening, being the first day of the week, when the doors were shut where the disciples were assembled for fear of the Jews, came Jesus and stood in the midst, and saith unto them, Peace be unto you" (John 20:19).*

7. *"And upon the first day of the week, when the disciples came together to break bread, Paul preached unto them, ready to depart on the morrow; and continued his speech until midnight" (Acts 20:7).*

8. *"Upon the first day of the week let every one of you lay by him in store, as God hath prospered him, that there be no gatherings when I come" (1 Cor. 16:2).*

As my parents studied these eight texts it soon became evident that the first five texts dealt with the resurrection of Jesus. Not one of them indicated that a worship service was taking place. These texts state that they came to the tomb after resting on the Sabbath to finish their work of taking care of the body of Jesus on the first day of the week. This was Sunday, a day for work and not worship. The sixth text states that the disciples were in a room with the doors bolted shut because they were afraid of what the Jews would do to them. The last two texts had to do with Paul preaching until midnight (Saturday evening). The Jewish day started with sunset and ended with the next sunset, therefore, Paul was preaching after sunset on the Sabbath, which made that the beginning of the first day of the week. In the morning he made his departure. The last text makes no mention of a religious meeting, but rather that the believers should remember to set aside an offering for Paul's work with the new believers.

The next Sunday morning my parents were ready with their questions that they would direct to their pastor. They were sure that he would be able to give them the right texts from the Bible that would help to straighten out Mr. Gossen. It was decided that Mother would meet with the pastor right after the church service so he would have more time to address this important topic. My parents had great respect for their pastor whom they had known for some time. My mother wrote down all the texts of the Bible that Mr. Gossen had given them in support of the biblical Sabbath. As soon as the church service was over and the pastor had finished greeting the parishioners, Mother took the opportunity to share her request with her beloved pastor. He politely listened to her, and when she had finished her presentation and asked for his help to direct her to some of the many texts in the Bible she thought must surely exist to prove that Sunday is the right day for worship, he sternly responded, "You need to respect your elders." She was so shocked and terribly disappointed. He was not able to give her a single text to support Sunday sacredness from the Bible. As she and my dad would discover in the next few weeks as they studied, there were none.

At their next Bible study with Mr. Gossen, my parents had to admit that they could not find a single text in the Bible that showed Sunday as the true day to worship God. Even their pastor was not able to help them.

Now there arose even more questions. If the seventh day of the week was the Sabbath of the Bible, or Saturday as the calendar has it, why are most Christians keeping Sunday? Further study revealed that the name Sunday originated from pagan worship of the sun god.

In the weekly cycle as we know it, the first day of the week is Sunday and Saturday is the seventh day of the week, which is the Sabbath. The order of the weekly cycle has not changed from the time that Jesus came to this earth. In the Bible, the day before the Sabbath was called the preparation day (*Mark 15:42*), or Friday as we know it today. The day after the Sabbath was the first day of the week (*Mark 16:1, 2*), or Sunday as we now know it, the day of Jesus' resurrection. One reason given among the Christian world for setting Sunday aside as a holy day of rest is in honor of Jesus' resurrection on Sunday morning. The Bible does say that He arose Sunday morning, but there is not a single verse in the Bible that states that the day is holy or that it is to take the place of the Sabbath. However, since all Protestant denominations have come from the Catholic Church who kept Sunday holy for hundreds of years before the Reformation of the fifteenth century and passed it on to most of the Christian world, they would most likely be able to provide the answer for the change. As my parents continued their study about the origin of Sunday as a day of rest in place of Saturday, Mr. Gossen showed them that the early Catholic Church made that change. *The Convert's Catechism of Catholic Doctrine,* by Rev. Peter Geiermann, has this to say about the change:

"Q. *Which is the Sabbath day?*
A. Saturday is the Sabbath day.

Q. *Why do we observe Sunday instead of Saturday?*
A. We observe Sunday instead of Saturday because the Catholic
Church transferred the Solemnity from Saturday to Sunday."[3]

During the course of my life I have often been asked, "Why make such a big deal about a day of worship?" "Does it really matter that much?" "Can't you worship God on any day of the week, a day that is more convenient to do so?" "You are out of step with the rest of the world because most Christians keep Sunday instead of the Bible Sabbath." In response

---

3   Peter Geiermann, The Convert's Catechism of Catholic Doctrine (St. Louis, MO: B. Herder Book Co, 1957), p. 50.

to these questions, we have explained that God has asked us to do it, and His commandments are more important than those of human devising. No one seems to have a problem with nine of God's commandments, only the one about the Sabbath. God has blessed us so much. He has preserved our life when we faced so many difficulties during the years of war. Why would we not trust and obey Him above any laws of church or state? We have endured much hardship and persecution, but God was always there to comfort and guide us when it seemed impossible to carry on. Why would we not put Him in first place in everything we do?

Although we were living in a restless world, the Sabbath was always a special day for our family. We knew that we were in harmony with God's requirements and had the privilege of praising Him for His care during times of hardship and persecution. We could not always trust our fellow man, but God was always there for us when we needed Him most.

This Bible study made a deep impression on both of my parents. They weighed the consequences on what the change from Sabbath to Sunday would mean in their relationship with their immediate family, friends and their community as a whole. They really had no arguments with anything Mr. Gossen had presented to them. All that he had taught them was backed up from the Word of God. My dad thought maybe they should just think about everything a little longer and then make their final decision when it felt right to do so. In the meantime, Mr. Gossen felt that my parents were not prepared to take such an important step and so he decided to postpone the Bible studies at least for a little while.

Mr. Gossen was not a man of great means and it actually was a great sacrifice for him to visit my parents on a weekly basis to study the Bible with them. He received no pay for these visits except if some people along the way would buy some of his books that he was hoping to sell. That was his only livelihood. It was also the winter season in Ukraine with deep snow drifts and extremely cold temperatures. During his visits with my parents they observed that he had neither boots nor even shoes, just slip-ons that were homemade. It soon became very obvious to my parents that he was a very dedicated man who felt compelled to share his Bible knowledge with them. The more my dad thought about everything that they had learned from the Bible in this short time and the dedication of this godly man as well as his own indecision to accept what they were taught, an uneasy feeling filled his heart. What if it was God that had sent this man to their door at this precise time? Would Mr. Gossen ever come back to them again or had he given up on them? My dad's mind was made up. He knelt down in prayer and said, "Lord, if You have sent this man to us and if You will impress him to return to us once more, I will accept the Sabbath because You have asked us to do so in Your Word." The very next week Mr. Gossen returned and my parents were convinced that God had sent him.

Since both of my parents had always put the teachings of the Bible above the authority of the church, it was now clear what their decision must be. They decided to follow God's Word rather than that of man. My mother made her decision right away while my dad decided to spend a little more time studying this subject more thoroughly. Then he too joined the little group that put the authority of the Bible above any teachings that were made by man. Their little church soon grew to about thirty members, and my father became its leader.

My parent's bee business. (left to right) My sister Lydia and Mother in the doorway

My father was a photographer by trade and was also a part-time bee-keeper, but whenever the opportunity presented itself, he would perform his pastoral duties to take care of our small church. The members of this little church were very active, and under my dad's leadership a good-sized orchestra was soon organized to be part of the worship service.

Dad's orchestra in his first organized church
(Dad and Mother in the middle row far right)

This was a time some years before World War II, and although religious freedom was not encouraged, it was tolerated for a few years yet. This was not the case in their tightly knit community of Mennonites, which included their own relatives and friends, who now shunned them for leaving their former church. But as far as my parents were concerned, God's requirements had to come first. These thorough studies of the Bible were a tremendous blessing to my parents. They studied topics such as the second coming of Jesus, the state of the dead, the resurrection, repentance, confession, Bible baptism, Bible prophecy and many other topics. My parents' faith in God was now stronger than ever which helped them in the years that would follow as World War II drew near.

Chapter 3

A Day to Remember

Civilian life in the Soviet Union during World War II was especially difficult. There was no way to escape the fierce fighting that surrounded the citizenry throughout each day and on through the night. Life was uncertain, and the expectation of something better faded like a well washed garment as one day fell into another. By this time, we had lost our home and there was no certainty from one day to the next where we would find shelter. Holding on one day at a time with the fear, anxiety and uncertainty of our circumstances, we focused on our immediate needs for survival.

Many people at this time lost their faith and trust in God, and the war brought out the worst in these individuals. In the daily deprivation of adequate food, homelessness, the relentless intense fighting and the fear of death, they could not see how God showed any concern for the affairs of this world. They became bitter and blamed God for the multitude of misery that they saw around them and helplessly endured.

There were grim consequences of the war that were heartbreaking, yet with no control over their situations, people were fated to endure whatever was thrust upon them. Perhaps especially hard was the knowledge that there were few people who could be trusted. Sadly, it was common for families to be separated from each other. The men were taken in one direction, and the women and children in another. Many of these families never heard from each other again even after the war was over. In many instances, the women were told that their husbands had been killed in battle. Eventually many of the women remarried, only to have their husbands return to them sometime later to find them married to another man. Many experiences, almost beyond human endurance, occurred on a daily basis. War was hell, and the devil was most certainly rejoicing over the carnage he was responsible for.

> *Since under communist rule religious freedom was denied, those who had the courage to maintain their faith and trust in God were severely punished. They were sent either to the inhumane concentration camps or put to death. As in the time of the Huguenots and Waldenses, religion had to go underground.*

Since under communist rule religious freedom was denied, those who had the courage to maintain their faith and trust in God were severely punished. They were sent either to the inhumane concentration camps or put to death. As in the time of the Huguenots and Waldenses, religion had to go underground. Unless you actually lived within the walls of communism, it would be difficult for one to understand what this meant. My father had an experience in the early years of communism that helped him understand more fully how deceitful it could be. Since we did not own a radio or television, we would go to the marketplace if we wanted to hear the latest news. The marketplace was filled with activity. You could find all manner of wares and foods that could be bought and sold by those who still had a bit of money. Here news traveled by word of mouth or you could purchase a newspaper to catch up, to some extent, on what was happening in the outside world. As my father made his way through the crowds, he passed a newsstand that sold newspapers. The large print headlines on the front page caught his attention. It boldly declared, "RUSSIA HAS RELIGIOUS FREEDOM." This was good news indeed. My father bought the paper with the idea that it would be useful if he were ever questioned by the authorities about our Sabbath worship. It would be a tremendous relief to worship within the law rather than in secret and not have to worry about the certain severe punishment if our Sabbath worship was revealed to the officials.

My father folded the newspaper, put it in his coat pocket and came home rejoicing. Now we could keep the Sabbath openly. It soon became known in our community that we were conducting religious services in our home. It also came to the attention of the Communist Party. Within a short time, a communist official showed up at our home one Sunday morning.

On answering the loud knock at the door, my father was confronted by an officer who brusquely asked, "Is it true that you conducted religious services in your home yesterday?" "Yes, sir," my father replied. "Are you not afraid to do so in view of the law we have that forbids this?" he asked. "No," my father replied as he showed the officer the paper he had bought the day before. The officer took the paper and turned it around facing away from him (indicating that it was written for the rest of the world), and said, "This we have written for them, but you should know better!" Then my father got the message—this was propaganda only. Russia wanted the free world to believe that it had religious freedom, when in actuality nothing had changed.

Yet God richly rewarded those who put their full trust and confidence in Him. It was in times like these that many encouraging and heart-warming experiences occurred that revealed God's love and leading through each intensely difficult day. Some believed that it was impossible to survive the terror of these times, but our heavenly Father did not forget His children who put their abiding trust in Him. It was during these most difficult years that our experience with our God reached an all-time high, never to be erased from our memories. With the sure knowledge that we serve a powerful God, our lives would never be the same again.

Since religious freedom was not sanctioned by the state, we did not have the option of worshipping with other believers in a church setting. In fact, all the churches were closed or used for purposes other than a house of worship. Many people who had completely given up their faith in God were the first ones to report those who still tried to gather together for worship services. We did not know whom we could trust so our services were held mostly in private homes with only two or three families. Even then great caution had to be taken so that undue attention was not drawn to our activities. It was arranged that one person would enter by way of the front door, and a few minutes later one or two would arrive at the back door. It was a matter of fact that we were always being watched by someone. It could be our neighbors who were against religious proceedings, or the police who kept a constant vigilance over any suspicious activity which they were required to report to the local Communist Party headquarters. At times, communist officials would randomly show up and investigate any unusual gathering. My uncle and his family sometimes met with our family in our home, but most of the time we were alone.

It was not only the lack of religious freedom, but the communist's disregard for any day of rest that compounded our already unstable situation. They had decreed that every day was a day for work, and they made sure that everyone was assigned work at a designated place. Communist officers would randomly check the residential areas to see if the people were home, or whether they were, in fact, at their assigned place of work. The communist philosophy was that every good communist was to productively support the state by working seven days a week. Though keeping the Sabbath day holy was most certainly not in line with communist ideology, the Hiebert household was determined to put the Lord first. We could not know at the time how He would answer our prayers. We felt somewhat like the three friends of Daniel when the king demanded them to worship the image of gold that he had erected. Their answer was like ours, *"Our God whom we serve is able to deliver us from the burning fiery furnace, and he will deliver us out of thine hand, O king. But if not, be it known unto thee, O king, that we will not serve thy gods, nor worship the golden image which thou hast set up"* (*Dan. 3:17, 18*). In our case, the image to be worshipped was communism and the fiery furnace was Siberia, a concentration camp or death by the firing squad.

We knew that the time would come soon enough when my father would be required to work at a job that would involve the Sabbath. Father called a family council meeting one morning and reviewed the challenges that we were then facing under communist rule. Our faith was strong in the Lord, but we were reminded that God expected us to do our part as well. We were convinced that we needed to escape from the Soviet Union for here we would never be permitted to worship according to the dictates of our conscience. It was agreed that a safe plan of escape needed to be executed as quickly as possible, one that would not entail taking major chances that would risk cutting short our lives. The escape plan had to take into consideration the length of time it could take to cover the long journey to West Germany. Most of this journey would be on foot, walking many kilometers each day. It would be imperative that we remain as inconspicuous as possible so that our intent would not be obvious to others. If it was discovered that we were trying to flee the country, there could be grave consequences. Another important point to be considered was the position of the battles of World War II. It seemed as if the fighting was raging everywhere across Europe. Thus, we had to choose a time and route for our escape that would not lead us into the hottest part of the war. Our inquiries as to where the fighting was most serious at that time caused us to realize that an escape at that particular juncture would be too risky. We made it a matter of prayer and waited for the Lord to show us when would be the best moment for us to make our move.

Our determination to be true to God regardless of the consequences included honoring the Sabbath day. Since this was not in harmony with the laws of the communist government, a bit of ingenuity had to be formulated. For a short time, we were living in a house (not our own) that had two windows with shutters in the front and a big door which served as the main entrance to the house. Whenever we left the house, we would secure the door with a big padlock. The padlock on the front door would indicate to any potential visitors, especially communist officers, that no one was expected to be home. Our Sabbath started on Friday at sunset and ended at sunset on Saturday. On Friday night one of the younger members of the family would go outside and put a big padlock on the front door after we were all in the house. This youngster would then be pulled up in through a window. The windows would then all be shut and the shutters securely bolted. We would then often forget the rest of the world around us until after the Sabbath hours. In the morning we would have our meager breakfast, then we would conduct our Sabbath worship. Always conscious of anyone that might be close to the house, we kept our voices low as we studied God's word and sang our praises to the One who sustained us day by day. After the noon meal we would engage in a thorough Bible study which would usually last the rest of the day. We did not have an

> *Our determination to be true to God regardless of the consequences included honoring the Sabbath day. Since this was not in harmony with the laws of the communist government, a bit of ingenuity had to be formulated.*

abundance of literature because the communists confiscated any religious material that they found, but we would sometimes exchange some small books or literature with my uncle and his family. There are many precious memories during that time of how the Lord protected us as we kept the Sabbath holy in an atheistic land.

One uncertain day passed into another, and each day we listened to the news, seeking information on the location of the battles hoping that the time had now come to make our move towards freedom. We had developed patience born through adversity and our trust in God as we waited until the site of the fighting shifted to a favorable position and a corridor opened up for our escape.

My father was the religious leader in our home, and he was also a pastor. Whether it was giving Bible studies, nurturing and visiting within our community or other activities in his role as pastor, he did so with the utmost caution. His official pastoral duties started on January 2, 1924, at twenty-seven years of age. However, this was not common knowledge as far as the communist government was concerned. His pastoral activities had to be done in secret for he knew that the communists were ever vigilant, watching our every move. If he were found out, punishment would be swift and severe.

Dad in World War II when we were separated
from him for six months

Professionally, my father was known in the community as a photographer. It would seem that the Lord had guided his life in this direction so that his work of ministry could continue. Even when the conditions at times seemed very dispiriting, the Lord always came through in a marvelous way. It was these difficulties and the Lord's answer to our prayers when we cried out to Him for help that served to further strengthen our faith and trust in Him. One such answer came on a Friday morning when we were startled to hear a loud knock at the door. In those days everyone except the communists lived in a continuous state of dread. We were still waiting for our chance of escape from communism and our fears were aroused. Had someone reported us? We were aware that most people would be very willing to report us to the authorities if it meant that they might benefit from doing so. The rule of life for most was, "Survival no matter what the cost." Opening the door, my father came face to face with a communist officer. "Are you Mr. Hiebert?" the officer questioned. "Yes, sir," my father replied. "I have heard about you and that you are a good photographer, one of the best." To this my father replied, "I always try to do my best work." "Yes," said the officer, "your best work you shall do. Starting tomorrow morning you are to report for work as the special photographer for the Communist Party office."

My father was caught off guard. What should his answer be? He could not refuse for that might be the end of any future plans of escape. What should he say? My father had a particular philosophy that he strictly adhered to: Never answer a question that you are not asked. This philosophy saved him from many potential problems before they became problems. My father also realized that "tomorrow morning" meant that the officer expected him to start his new job on the Sabbath. It is in times like these when we trust the Lord completely that He puts words in our mouth that astound us. After a few seconds of reflection, which at the time seemed like hours, my father replied, "Sir, you want me to do my very best for you as a photographer. When I receive an important assignment as this, I need a day to prepare myself for it." The officer was not expecting this kind of an answer. He looked very displeased at first, but after a moment of reflection as he considered my father's response, he agreed. Apparently, he deemed it a reasonable request for the important job he expected my father to be in charge of. Before leaving, he said, "But Sunday morning I want you to show up and report to me." "Yes, sir," said my father. And with that, he was gone.

Not only was my father commanded to work as a photographer for the Communist Party but on his first day of work he was also to bring his appointment book with him that he had used prior to his new work for the communists. In this book were all the names of the people that had their pictures taken by my dad. His assignment was to check on all these people if they were capitalists or had people working for them. The communists frowned on anyone who had servants/employees working for them which put them in the category of being a capitalist. All these people my dad was to report to the communist chief and they would then be promptly loaded on trains or trucks and sent off to Siberia. Of course, my father had no intention of reporting his former clients, but not doing so would put him on the list to be sent to Siberia. What should he do? He was in a no-win situation. The whole matter weighed heavily on his mind. There was only one solution, God was the only One that could help him in this terrible predicament. He earnestly sought the Lord to intervene on his behalf and that of his clients. On the day that he was to report all these people to commit them to a life in Siberia, he did not give his report and the Lord caused the chief to forget that he had asked my dad to do so. The chief never brought it up again and Dad thanked the Lord for saving him from this terrible situation.

Always foremost in our minds were our plans to escape to freedom. It now seemed as if these plans would have to be put on hold until the Lord would reveal to us a better time. After all, the Lord had just answered our prayer. Father had been given permission to be home tomorrow which was the Sabbath. It would truly be a day of preparation that would give us strength for the following week. What a delight it was to know that we could keep the Sabbath, knowing that the communists would not check on us or expect my father to show up for work on that day. We worshipped on the first Sabbath with the communist's permission, so to speak, and our trust in the Lord grew ever stronger. Sometimes the Lord leads step by step, not always as we expect, but always leading through difficult times.

After the Sabbath was over, Sunday came all too quickly. The future safety of our family was uncertain, but at family worship that Sunday morning we left everything in God's hands. On Sunday morning Father set out for work as required.

Upon his arrival, Father was given an orientation of the place where he was to work and specific instructions on how he was to carry out his duties. There were long steps leading up to the front of the building to the main entrance. At one end of a lengthy hallway there were various offices on one side, and one large office on the other side which was to be my father's office and place of work. At the other end of the hallway was the office of the communist officer. In order to get to his workplace, it was necessary for him to pass the office where my father would be working. My father's workspace had three walls with a lot of windows. This was in the days before fluorescent lighting and since his work required a brightly lit room for him to perform his best work, it was felt that this was the ideal place in the building for him. Most of the work he did was black and white photography. Colored photos were rare but, if requested, he would touch up the black and white photos with oil pencil crayons to reflect the true colors of the picture. Often, when people were being photographed, he would have them posed before him as he touched up the photos to reflect the color of their clothing, hair and complexion. With today's technology, his work would have been much simpler.

Included in the orientation were specific instructions regarding my father's relationship to the communist officer and the conditions he was to follow in performing his duties. The officer curtly spelled out his duties: "I will give you a key to this room, and only you and I will have keys to this room. When you are not in the room, or when you leave your place of work in the evening to return to your home, you are to lock this room because there is a lot of valuable material and equipment which we need to keep safe. We have supplied you with the equipment and material needed for your work: various types of cameras, tripods, film, different kinds of paper, oil-based pencil crayons for touch up work, etcetera. In the evening, before you leave for home, you need to put everything in its rightful place. Everything has a place and everything must be put in its place. The work that you will be doing in this office is strictly confidential. You will be taking pictures of some of the communist leaders and their families and, in some cases, operations in progress in the hospital where it involves some of these communist leaders. Is that understood?" "Yes, sir," my father replied.

The reason for the photography in the hospital was that they did not always trust the doctors; therefore, they wanted to have all the necessary evidence documented in case of foul play. Distrust of anyone and everything was the order of the day. One time, during the course of his work at that office, the communist officer asked him to come with him to a large auditorium. There on the stage, with its fully opened curtain, were numerous skeletons. On the far left there was a skeleton of an ape and on the far right that of a human and in between the gradual development of ape to human. The communist leader then turned to my father and said, "I want you to take a picture of our forefathers." Of course, he did as he was told, but his thoughts were, *They might be your forefathers, but I certainly don't claim them as mine.*

With the orientation and instructions behind him, my father began to set up his office and start on his assignments. Being quite a perfectionist, my father took his work of photography seriously. He worked on through the rest of the day without encountering any more visits from the communist chief. It was usual for this officer to come to work in mid-morning and leave work in the middle of the afternoon. You could say he had banker's hours. Because of his abbreviated hours he was usually not in the office when my father arrived and was gone when my father returned home. At the end of his first day of work my father put all his material and equipment in their rightful places as requested, locked the door to his office, and came home.

The first day of work was uneventful; however, Father had not given up on our plan to escape to West Germany. We continually kept ourselves updated on the position of the fighting, and it was our plan to immediately leave the area as soon as it was safe to do so. It was our belief that this could happen any day and possibly within that very week. Our journey to freedom would take many days and there was always the possibility of being detected. For many a risk like this was not worth it, but we could not see ourselves staying in the Soviet Union living in fear every day for the rest of our lives. Our hopes for escape that particular week soon diminished as one day turned into another with Friday and another Sabbath rapidly approaching. My father earnestly pled with the Lord and asked another Adventist family to join us in prayer appealing to the Lord to protect us from the threats of the communist authorities.

As the sun set on Friday evening and the Sabbath began, my father never once considered going to work the next morning even though we still had no sign of how the Lord would intervene. God had marvelously interceded on the first Sabbath and Father's determination never wavered. We would honor the Sabbath with or without the approval of the communist officer, come what may. As my father went to work that Friday morning, he prayed that the Lord would give him the right words when approaching the officer. However, that opportunity did not avail itself and we kept the Sabbath without the officer's permission.

On Sunday morning father went to work in fear, not knowing what to expect. He said goodbye to his family in the event that he would never see us again. Approaching his office, he unlocked the door and prepared all of his equipment for work. Following his philosophy "not to answer questions that you are not asked," he did not volunteer an explanation to anyone in the office as to why he was not at work the previous day. This philosophy had saved him on many occasions during the course of his life, and especially while under communist rule. Presently, however, the communist chief came by, and seeing my father at work said, "Mr. Hiebert, it was probably too dark for you to work yesterday and therefore you did not come to work." At first my father did not know what he was talking about, but on further reflection he remembered that on Sabbath it had been very cloudy and extremely dark. When the chief did not see my father at work that day, he reasoned to himself that since my father required strong lighting to do an acceptable job for him, and because it was very dark that Sabbath, my father did not feel it necessary to come to the office. It did not take long for my father to respond affirmatively. In our family, to this day we remember the second Sabbath as the "Dark Day." God is so good. Again, He had answered our prayers in a way we had not expected.

Every day the following week my father went to work in the hope that a way might possibly open up for us to start on our escape that week. Yet as the days slipped by, drawing closer to another Sabbath, he realized that the plans for an escape would have to be put on hold. God had helped him in a marvelous way on the first two Sabbaths, and we would continue to trust Him with our lives.

On Friday evening before coming home, my father cleaned up his office, putting everything in its proper place as required. As he was about to lock the door, the communist chief came down the hallway from his office and said, "Mr. Hiebert, tomorrow is a very special day." Of course, my father could fully agree with that since it was the Sabbath, but he waited to hear why the chief thought it was a special day. "Tomorrow is a very

> *We safely kept the third Sabbath and rejoiced in the fact that the Lord had answered our prayers so quickly. Sabbath number three will always be remembered by our family as the "Sabbath of the Communist Party Meeting."*

special, confidential communist meeting in this building, and we want no one else, including you, to show up here. Is that understood?" Overjoyed, my father quickly responded, "Yes, sir." We safely kept the third Sabbath and rejoiced in the fact that the Lord had answered our prayers so quickly. Sabbath number three will always be remembered by our family as the "Sabbath of the Communist Party Meeting."

As we entered into the fourth week again hoping that this was the week we could start our journey to freedom, the days came and went in a familiar pattern. Friday was soon upon us and with it the challenge of not working on Sabbath. My father now understood that as far as the communists were concerned there was absolutely no valid excuse to have Sabbath off from work. It would be useless to ask for the day off or try to think of an excuse not to show up. The only possible help was from the Lord.

On the fourth Friday Father showed up for work just as he did on every other Friday morning. There was not a doubt in his mind that the Lord could help him as in the past, but he couldn't imagine how it might happen. Sabbath number one was "A Day of Preparation," Sabbath number two was a "Dark Day," Sabbath number three was "The Communist Party Meeting." What other possibility was left? All through that day my father wondered what he could say or do in preparation for the oncoming Sabbath, but nothing came to mind.

As the end of the workday drew near that Friday, it was clear to him that unless God performed another miracle, his fate was in the hands of the Communist Party chief. He knew without a shadow of a doubt that outside of the Lord's intervention, his future looked hopelessly bleak. He was convinced, however, that he could not expect the Lord to come to his rescue unless he had done his part. Following the communist chief's strict instructions, he made absolutely sure that everything in his office was in order with everything in its proper place before he left for home. Casting one final, careful glance around the room, he locked the door to his office and made his way along the long hallway and down the lengthy span of steps heading for home. But no! He felt compelled to go back one more time to double-check his efforts making sure nothing was amiss that the communist chief could use against him. He retraced his steps and unlocked his office door. Carefully reviewing the entire room, he was satisfied that he had left no reason that the chief could use against him when he returned to work on Sunday morning. Having satisfied himself that he had done his part, he again locked the door and came home to keep the fourth Sabbath.

On Sunday morning he went to work as usual, unsure of what he would be facing. Approaching his office door, he was disturbed to find it not only unlocked, but wide open. All of his cameras and equipment that he used for his work were placed as though he had been working and had put nothing away when he left for home on Friday. Yet he knew that was not the case. Deeply puzzled, he was unable to make any sense of what was before him. Thoughts ran through his mind. Had the communist chief decided to replace him, and then deal with him later? Why was the equipment in the room placed in the exact location as he would be accustomed to placing it had he been at work? All these and other questions streamed through his mind. But seeing no one else in the room and no sign of the chief, he decided to continue on with his work as usual.

He was deeply involved with his work when the communist chief hurried past his office door, then stopped and retraced his steps. Standing in the doorway he declared in a stern voice, "My friend, when you stop for lunch you need to lock your office door because there is valuable equipment in there that could be stolen." "Yes, sir," replied my father. The chief disappeared as quickly as he had appeared, leaving my father in a dazed state of confusion. What had just happened? What was he talking about? All through that day my father mulled over the strange experience of that morning. The only people who had a key to his office were the chief and himself. Obviously, the chief had not been in his office, having no reason to be there since he knew nothing about photography, and my father was at home observing the Sabbath. But who had unlocked his office door? Who took all of the equipment out of the cupboards and placed it exactly as my father would have had he been at work? My father determined that these are the first questions he wants to ask his guardian angel in the kingdom of heaven. The Lord has ways to protect His children when they find themselves in straight and difficult places that causes one to feel most humble.

My father finally surmised, right or wrong, that when the chief came to work that Sabbath morning, he had noticed my father's office door unlocked and wide open. As he looked into the room, he saw all the equipment in place as though my father was at work. However, since he did not see my father, he assumed that he had gone for lunch and forgot to lock his office door. Evidently this must have been the only time he passed by my father's office that day. Isn't it amazing what the Lord will do when we trust Him supremely?

An acquaintance of my father also had a special Sabbath experience. He was working along with many other workers when he was asked to labor on a particular Sabbath. During that day his boss had apparently looked for him, but did not see him, and later forgot to continue looking for him. All the while our brother was at home keeping the Sabbath. On Sunday morning he was back at work, and when his boss saw him, he stated, "I did not see you here at work yesterday." "No," replied our brother, "I did not see you either." I can't help but think that the Lord has a delightful sense of humor, even in times where everything seems less than humorous to us.

Leaving our home where I was born in Halbstadt, Ukraine, 1943, in an open train car. I am in the front and the rest of my family are behind me. I was three years old. We were separated from Dad at this time.

The day finally came during the following week when we were able to begin our escape from that part of the Ukraine on our way to Poland. Throughout this uncertain and threatening time, we never missed keeping the Sabbath. Thankfully, some of the Sabbaths were less dramatic than others, but we always knew that whatever peril we were facing, the Lord would never forget about us. When we finally escaped to West Germany years later, some of our members who had also escaped from several of the areas where we had been, said to us, "Now we can start keeping the Sabbath again." To this my father humbly replied, *"We have never missed a Sabbath."*

Chapter 4
Years Without Dad

There is a certain poignancy that is felt when a firsthand account is presented of events that one has undergone through distressing circumstances. Following is a letter written by my mother to a family friend dated July 8, 1946. As you will see, she has shared many of the experiences that our family encountered during the last three years of the war. This was the time when our father was taken from us, and we were without his support, encouragement and wise leadership. After reading this account, one of Mother's friends sent this letter to a German periodical where it was published in 1954. I have translated the letter and present it now as an authentic picture from my mother's standpoint as to how the war years and our refugee life affected her while she was forcibly separated from her husband.

Dear Friends,

God's peace and grace be with you all. Since many have already written to you, I also would like to share with you our experiences of the past few years. I will try to be as brief as possible; otherwise I could write many pages.

On December 11, 1944, we were separated from my dear husband and father of our children. On January 20, 1945, we left the area where we last lived as a family. Three days later, on January 23, we arrived at the main railroad station. From that time on the authorities made the decisions as to where to send everyone. Some were sent in one direction and some in another. We had no choice in the matter. We arrived at a country manor, along with a number of other families. The train that we were traveling on was an open train car, and due to the extremely cold January weather my ten-year-old son Arthur and I suffered with frozen toes while on this three-day trip. For about a month after, we both experienced excruciating pain in our feet.

When we arrived at the manor we were given one nice room in the attic that met all of our needs. We thanked the Lord that He had protected us and given us a place to rest. Shortly after we arrived, five-year-old Jacob had the measles, however, it was not a severe case and did not last too long.

In just one week after our arrival, the big storm of the war caught up with us. The women and younger girls were in the greatest danger. I was very fearful for my eighteen-year-old daughter Erna, and I suffered great anxiety and fear over what might happen to her from the soldiers. At first, she hid herself with the other girls, but when this did not work anymore, she would get into bed and pretend that she was sick. Most of the soldiers accepted that as a good enough reason to leave her alone. There were others, however, who did not let any excuse keep them from molesting the girls.

Since Erna actually was suffering with a heart condition, her health worsened because of the terrible fear of what might happen to her. She would break out in a heavy sweat and could barely speak. I was afraid that she would die. We resolutely turned to God and pled with Him for help and to protect us. As we look back on those times, we can now thank Him for answering our prayers. He did not permit our only daughter to be molested. Thank God, His name be praised.

In our little room by my bed was a wall hanging with a crocheted picture of a large angel with his wings spread out, and on the side were the words *Gott halt in Gnaden treue Wacht, in diesem Hause Tag und Nacht* [God in grace keeps true watch, in this house day and night]. Time after time this was a true comfort to us as we daily experienced His care over us.

After each family had been given a place to live at this manor, the authorities decided to send all the girls to various places for work, and the women were sent to work in the farmers' fields. We were not able to bring much food with us on the trip, and most people did not care much about us refugees. Now again, we turned to our heavenly Father to take care of our physical needs. Our trust was in Him, and He did not disappoint us.

He daily took thought to have our needs met, as a father takes care of his children.

An older soldier now came to us two or three times every day. My sister Anna and I had to pump water for his big water tank which he then had to bring to a mill. For our service, he gave us some bread to eat, enough for each day. We also had some potatoes. During this time, my sister Anna and I went every day to the fields since our soldier who had supplied us with bread had gone away. But before he left, he felt sorry for us and gave us a whole bag of whole wheat flour. Erna was now able to bake bread for all of us as needed. We were also able to secure some sugar beets from the fields which provided us with some syrup. We were especially overjoyed when we were able take care of a cow for a short while, which gave us access to all the milk that we needed.

It was very interesting how we ended up with the cow. During the course of the war when the farmers were driven away from their farms, their animals were left to fend for themselves in fields and barns. As times became more serious and food was not available, some of the soldiers gathered up these cows in order to use them for their food later on. They drove these cows long distances from one village to another, after which the poor animals were famished and dehydrated, and some of them would collapse when they could go no further. That, of course, was the case with our particular cow. The soldiers hit the cow, but the cow could not get up. Arthur then approached one of the soldiers and said, "Do you want me to take care of the cow?" The soldier was delighted, and agreed that he could do anything he wanted to with the cow as she was only a hindrance to him at the time. Continuing on with the rest of the cows, he left the cow to Arthur to take care of. My children then found a place in a small barn next to where we lived for the cow, and took care of her as best as they could. It was obvious that the cow had suffered extensively from this long trip, but since it was a young cow, she soon responded to the love that she received from my children, and they decided to milk the cow. At first she hardly produced a liter of milk, but in time she produced up to nine liters each milking. With all this milk, we were able to share with others around us who could not begin to dream of faring so well during the time of war. Of course, we also had other by-products from the milk; we separated the cream from the milk and made butter, and also made cottage cheese, and for a short time we were able to eat like kings. Some of these milk products we were even able to take with us when we suddenly had to leave this area to move on. This supplied us with food for another couple of days until we could find something else.

Bit by bit Erna slowly recovered, and instead of being bedridden she took care of more of the household chores as she was able. She was very frugal and was able to make the meals as we still had quite a bit of butter and milk. When we came in from the fields very tired, she had everything ready so we could be strengthened with a good meal.

There was no one in this area that we were acquainted with, but as we stepped off the train in January, we suddenly met our dear friend Lena. Our joy was short-lived, however, as with all the many refugees, we soon lost track of her. Some of the people from our manor were suddenly loaded up and taken away. We did not know where they went, but were told that they were going home (that could mean that they may have been sent to Siberia). We were also supposed to be loaded up on the train cars, but before we could board the train we were told that there was no more room. So we, our family and two other women, were left behind.

One Friday as we came home from our work in the fields, we were surprised to find our friend Lena in our room. We were so overjoyed to see her again. She told us that she had been placed in the village next to ours. We were forced to go to work every day, and God gave us the strength to do so. We were also able to keep every Sabbath at home. Sometimes, the authorities had a great need for our help on Sabbath, and when we did not go to work the superintendent would be in a rage, and he would threaten to take our cow and all of our food away, leaving us with nothing if we did not work on Sabbath. However, I was quite at peace and thought everything is in God's hands. He had helped us so many times when we were in the greatest need, and surely He would not leave us now. The next day we went to work as usual, and no one asked us any questions.

During this time we would visit with our friend Lena in the next village, and she would visit with us when possible. Since we were in the country, we started a little garden planting potatoes and various kinds of vegetables. We were here in this place until July 4, 1945.

After this, while we were in Poland, the news came to us that the Polish people would drive all Germans out of their towns and cities. Since we received this information ahead of time, we decided to start on our journey the day before. It was a dark night with heavy rain. The rain continued all through the night and into the next day. We traveled with our friend Lena and several other families. Together, we were able to secure a wagon and an ox to hitch to it. The youngest children were permitted to ride on the wagon when they became too tired to walk. We did not get far before the ox and wagon were taken from us, and most of the food that we had taken with us stayed on the wagon, as well as books that I had taken along.

We also had made ourselves a small wagon that we pulled by hand, but it soon broke apart since it was of a woman's devising. The second day at noon, the heavy rain had stopped and the sun began to shine.

We were drenched and now took a little time to rest and change into dry clothes, making our little bundle that we carried much smaller as we had to throw some of the clothes away that we could not use anymore. We then continued our march forward. After we had gone thirty kilometers and were extremely tired, we sought a place where we could spend the night. We found grace at a certain place and were also offered a little bread. Moving on we came to an empty school building with a barn. We went to the barn and picked up a lot of straw which we would use as a mattress for our night's rest.

When I awoke the next morning, I could not move my limbs because of the severe pain. I was stiff and full of pain and cried, "I cannot go any farther." However, with the help of my dear children, we pulled ourselves together and joined the others who were ready to continue on the journey. We had to leave our flour, breakfast foods and sugar behind, but we still had bread and lots of our treated butter. We were still able to eat well, and after we ate and were strengthened, our journey continued. Due to the long and tiresome walk, we had to leave a lot of things behind as we were too tired to carry them.

Our friend Lena had a wheelbarrow where she had loaded all kinds of food and dishes and clothing, but after many kilometers of walking and pushing the wheelbarrow, she finally concluded, "You will see, I will soon throw my wheelbarrow with everything in it into the ditch, and then I will be free from this burden. Whatever we need, God will again supply." As our travels continued, our provisions grew less and less. Our feet were aching from the long walk, and our arms were sore from carrying what we still possessed. As much as possible, we would try to be positive, encouraging and helping one another as we slowly went on our way.

Mother and Jacob

Our Jacob was quite willing to put up with everything with the under-
standing that someone would take him by the hand and, if possible, pull
him along a little bit. He especially wanted to be close to me. That was
hard because I could not say no to him. After we had traveled a consider-
able distance, Arthur discovered a small wagon along the way. He fixed it
up a bit and tied Jacob's bundle of clothes to the wagon. Excited, he now
pulled the wagon in a gallop, way ahead of all of us, hopping and jumping
as if this was the first day of our travels.

Even though we put many kilometers behind us every day with very little time to rest, we noticed that our joints were not as stiff as when we first started out. By the end of the second week, we arrived at the Oder, a big river in Europe. We were very fearful over the news that we received. Here the Polish authorities decided to separate many families in order to secure a work force that they required. Again God came to our rescue, and our family was allowed to stay together. Many of those that we had set out with on our travels were able to travel faster than I and my family could, so we were no longer together. Now it was just our friend Lena and ourselves. We walked every day, but on Sabbath we did not. In due time, another lady and her son joined us. This lady was very tired and asked our friend Lena to go with her to see if she could board a train to visit her brother. Now I was all alone with my family and felt totally abandoned by everyone. I felt more deserted than ever before in my life. Our food supply that we had taken with us was now gone, and we were at the mercy of whatever people might give us.

It was Friday and the sun was sinking in the west as we arrived in a larger city begging for some food, but the people gave us nothing. They had potatoes in the stores, but now all the stores were closed. I continually prayed to God for assistance that He might help us out of this great dilemma. I then took a container and went to get water. As I crossed the road, I looked up and saw several wagons loaded with potatoes coming my way. I ran with my container and begged for a few potatoes, and my request was granted. I quickly went with the container of potatoes to my family, rejoicing and thankful that my God was there to help, and yet ashamed of my lack of faith. Now I made my way again to get water. As I did so, another wagon with potatoes came by. The man gave me a subtle sign for me to jump on the wagon and fill my container with potatoes. He helped me to fill it as much as possible, and I then jumped off the wagon as he continued on. Now we had enough potatoes for the evening, and also for the whole Sabbath. The next day, in the meadows we saw a large heard of cows that had been driven there, so Erna and I went and milked the cows. We were then given a little place where we could spend the night and Sabbath, and we thanked God for His goodness This experience I will never forget and it greatly strengthened my faith for the rest of my life.

The next day we were back on the road again. You might ask what kind of a house did you stay in? We usually found shelter at night as we were going from one town to the next in buildings that were half bombed, or in barns. We would cook our meals under the open sky on two stones.

Now we came to another town where it seemed that we might be able to board a train. What good news that would be. The train was so full, however, that there was no room for any of us or anyone else. There were some people who decided to hang on to the side of the train, and asked us to do the same.

However, we were very fearful to do so for we feared that one of our family might fall off and be injured or lose their life, so we carried on with our walking—one kilometer at a time. Each day we put behind us less kilometers than the day before because we were exhausted from the long pilgrimage. Jacob now began to complain as well; he said that all of his bones were about to break and he asked, "When will God give us a house again?" We tried to encourage him to buoy him up. I then became very sick and could not continue on for a day, however, the next day we slowly continued to go a little further.

Finally, the Polish authorities decided to put one hundred refugees in a big house that used to be considered a mansion. Now we were expected to work again, and the authorities paid no attention to the fact that we had been on the road so long and were in a very weakened condition. If we did not work, we would receive no bread. Those that worked received a little bit of bread, and for the noon and evening meals a thin potato soup was provided. My sister Anna and Erna were active in several types of duties in the kitchen. One day both of them came home totally drenched from the rain, and the next day both of them were very sick in bed. Erna regained her strength in a couple of days, but my sister Anna had the severe disease of typhus with a high fever. She did not eat and became very weak. Our children then went to people in the village and begged for a little food for her. She was so sick that she at first refused to eat, however, with much encouragement she ate a little of the food that they brought. She was in bed for six weeks slowly recovering and regaining her strength. Many of the people who stayed where we were had the same sickness and a number of them died. Since there were so many people in this house, and there was much sickness because the people were so weak, there was a big epidemic of lice, like I have never seen in my life. The older people usually did not survive. They became discouraged, laid down in their bed, and their life ended in a pitiful way amid much pain and suffering. Almost every day dead people were taken out of this big house. During the time that we spent in this deserted mansion, thirty people died. We were twenty people in one room, and it is all that we could do to keep ourselves free from the lice that were everywhere.

When my dear husband and our children's father was separated from us and we said goodbye to him, we were overwhelmed to think that we might never see each other again. We agreed at that time that if we could not find each other, we would both resort to writing to our church headquarters in Berlin in search of each other once the war had ended. As soon as we were aware that the mail delivery was somewhat restored, we sent a letter to Berlin, inquiring whether anyone had heard of David Hiebert. Time passed with no reply. Now we were very sad. During this time, people who were looking for their missing family members would send letters to a certain area or through the Red Cross, and if both letters arrived they would put one letter into the other and send that letter to the family member, and it would help them to locate each other. After everything that we had experienced so far, our greatest worry now was for my husband and father of my children. Where might he be and when would we find each other? The children at times said, "Maybe he is dead already." But to that I replied very emphatically, "No, I have a strong faith and trust in God that he is still alive, and we will be reunited again."

Since we received no word from our letters for quite a while, we thought that maybe in Berlin everything had been destroyed through the war, and therefore our letters were not going through. In that case, God could help us in a different way since we heard from some people how some had suddenly found each other. From time to time I said to Erna, "We should try to write again; maybe the first letter got lost." However, she was too discouraged, and so for a while we did not write. It was during this time that Arthur had a big sore on his chest which caused him great pain.

Many of the people residing where we did as refugees decided to continue their walk to see if they could find better accommodations. We also would have liked to leave this area, but my sister Anna, after her severe sickness, was still very weak so we could not continue our journey. It was now getting a little colder. We slept just on straw and had only a thin blanket, as well as our coats to cover us. God's help, however, always came at the right time. In a wonderful way we were able to secure a big feather bed and three pillows, a new blanket, and a few other things. We also were given a little room for only our family, rather than sharing one room with twenty people. As the winter weather came, our situation improved a bit and we received a little bit of food. We had a stove in our room, and since wood was available we were able to cook and heat with the wood and were able to keep warm. So we decided to stay here for the winter. We also continued to look for my husband, but without success.

At the beginning of February, the lily of the valley began to bloom and new life began to show up in nature. But our hope to have our family reunited was still far from reality. We cried a lot and felt very alone. I was glad when Erna went to work because she would then not have time to think, for the doctor said that anxiety would be very hard on her already sick heart.

> *One day as Erna came home from work, she was unusually full of courage. "You know, Mother," she said, "this evening I will again write a letter to Berlin and you will see that Dad will also send a letter there and our letters will meet, and then we will find each other."*

One day as Erna came home from work, she was unusually full of courage. "You know, Mother," she said, "this evening I will again write a letter to Berlin and you will see that Dad will also send a letter there and our letters will meet, and then we will find each other." "Oh yes," I replied, "I've often said we should write again. Let's try it again one more time." The same evening she finished her letter, and the next day she sent it as registered mail. At once we figured out when we could expect an answer, or when the letter would come back. However, to our dismay, we received no letter and neither did the letter come back. Now we did not know what to think any more.

At this time, many people decided to travel to the West, so we also decided that in a few days we would join another family and start on our trip West as well. In the meantime, it was Friday. My sister Anna and Erna came home for dinner and after we had eaten, a lady suddenly came to our door and cried, "Come quickly, outside there is a man who is asking for the Hieberts." Full of surprise and hope, we ran down the steps. Erna was already far ahead and was the first to greet him. Even though he was still a distance away from the house, I soon realized it was my David! We greeted each other with joy and tears. Now that we were all together, it seemed to us as though it was a dream, but it was actually reality. He brought many presents with him; raisins and figs and other dried fruits, which no one could expect to find during this time. We thanked the Lord for His love and grace and wonderful way He led us back together, and we all joined in a song in German which stated, "The Lord has done great things for us, therefore we are happy and thankfulness is fitting to be made, and our rejoicing reaches to the heavens above ...." It actually happened according to the great faith that Erna had. She wrote to Berlin and my husband also wrote and both letters were put together. My husband received both letters and brought them with him as he made his way to locate us.

He had now come to take us to where he had been assigned to work. We decided, however, that we should go to the West to find freedom, rather than stay in the East. Father arrived on March 8 and on March 12, 1946, we left this area. Our travels took us very close to where my husband had been working, and since he had left some of his belongings there, we decided to stop by his place of work for a short time and continue on to freedom the next day. However, my husband's boss pled with us not to leave so quickly so we decided to stay for a little while, and continue our trip westward after a few weeks.

Signed,
Your Sister in the Lord, Lena (Helene)

Many years have gone by since our family experienced what my mother so graphically described in her letter. Now, as an adult, I can better understand the stress and anguish that she was forced to endure as she supported and protected her flock of five souls. I marvel that she was able to survive such an ordeal. It could only have been her strong faith in God, her supremely unselfish love for her family and God's direct intervention and protection that can explain how it was possible for each of us to live through those years when so many others fell victim to the cruelties and neglects inflicted during these war years.

Even though we eventually left behind us the years of war with its anxieties, fears, diseases and severe famine, there were consequences. My dear mother's health was seriously affected. The life of a refugee during the course of over five years while living in the midst of the fiercest fighting of World War II had left its effects. My parents actually lived through both world wars where both of these wars were being fought. In each, they were helplessly caught in the middle where the fiercest action of the war in that region took place.

As one who was by her side through a number of those wretched years, I can attest to the fact that my mother faced the battles of life that were forced upon her bravely and with an unwavering faith. Sadly, she did not live long to enjoy the years of freedom in the country we now call home, Canada. At the age of sixty-one, after a lengthy illness, she passed to her rest. She now awaits the coming of Jesus, when all wars, pain and sorrows will be no more. Had it not been for her unselfish love for her family, I would not have survived to render this marvelous account of how God brought us through the storms of life.

Chapter 5

Protection in Crisis

Our family faced many trials and challenges that sorely tried our faith during the time when we were separated from our father. We were separated twice from him. The Russians separated the men from their families to be employed at their will either in the war or labor camps. The women were usually sent to work on government farms harvesting farm produce. Any separations were done at the will of the government and my dad had no choice in the decision. However, he never carried arms.

The first separation forced upon our family by the communists lasted for six months in 1943. We were living in a town called Halbstadt (in Ukraine) where I was born. The second time we were separated from our father was on December 11, 1944, and it wasn't until March 8, 1946, that we were once again reunited as a family. This was the longest separation from him lasting for a year and three months. It was a dark and difficult time as it often appeared as if we would never see him again. The reports coming out of the war were not encouraging, and as it turned out thousands of families had to accept that they would never again be reunited with their loved ones.

We were now on our own without Dad's wise counsel, encouragement and care. Mother was now the head of our household, and we came to see as never before how strong and deep a faith she possessed. Whatever challenges the day would bring our way, whether intense fear, hunger, the extreme cold of a winter with no shelter, threats from the soldiers, exhaustion after walking seemingly endless kilometers a day, Mother handled all of these trials with amazing strength. That is not to say that the years of war didn't take a heavy toll on her health, shortening her life once the storm was over and we were in a land of freedom. Often, when confronted with unwelcome circumstances, it seems that there is an inner strength that we draw from that enables us to endure more than we thought possible. I found this to be true not only of my mother, but also of my sister Erna, and my brother Arthur. As I look back on those years, I can clearly see how each member of our family rose to the occasion when the situation demanded it. Even so, without God's guidance and loving care all our efforts would have been of no benefit.

During most of the years of World War II, and several years thereafter, we were known as refugees. Only those who have at one time been a refugee will understand what that means. Refugees do not have a permanent home and never know from one day to the next where they may be. There were many times when we would walk up to thirty kilometers a day, and when we stopped at evening, hungry and bone weary, we had to look for a place to spend the night. If we were fortunate, we might find a house where its owners or fellow refugees had vacated when they were forced to move on, or we might settle for a house that had been bombed with a few walls and part of the roof still intact that provided a meager but welcome cover from the elements. At other times, we would find shelter in a barn. When we were forced to stay in a place for a longer period of time and the authorities had a bit of compassion for human life, we were put in empty storage houses, auditoriums or other buildings with large rooms. At times, we were placed in a regular sized room with twenty people, all of whom were strangers to us. On several occasions, we were placed in a large auditorium with over 100 people who occupied the same large space. Privacy was not an option.

It was a time of great uncertainty and weariness for refugees as they could not make plans for each day. It was always the authorities or the conditions that dictated what would transpire for them that day. If they endeavored to plan their days, they needed to be prepared to abandon their ideas at a moment's notice, day or night. There were times when they would be at a particular place for only a day or be forced to stay put for a few weeks or even months. When forced to be on the move, those that were severely sick or exhausted from trudging the many miles days on end received no sympathy from the authorities. They were expected to be on the move until their feeble strength gave out, or they took their last faltering breath. No time was allowed for a decent funeral. The dead were merely wrapped in a blanket, if one was available, and placed in a hastily dug grave that the next of kin or friends had quickly prepared. They were buried and left behind with no time to mourn their loss or mark their last resting place. One can only imagine the silent tears and sweet memories of better times that the survivors mutely bore as they moved forward into their own uncertain future.

Refugees did not have the luxury of going to the supermarket to buy provisions for each day. If there were any stores that had survived the bombings, there was little or no food there. Even when there was food available it was of no consequence to us as we had little or most often no money to buy anything. When times were desperate, we would beg for food from those that were fortunate to still be landowners and possessed a bit of produce they could share. It was common when staying at a place for a few weeks or even months, for all able-bodied, or most of the time not too able-bodied, to be required to work for the Russians in the fields or in their army kitchens. In most cases they received no pay, but were given a third of a small loaf of bread for a day's work. This was then brought home and shared with their children or family members who were too sick or weak to work. A scant sustenance that failed to assuage the hunger that relentlessly gnawed away at scores of malnourished civilians.

In view of the uncertainties of our status as refugees, we endeavored to follow a long-range plan whenever possible that would bring us ever closer to West Germany and freedom. Our plans were often fraught with delays or adjustments depending on the conditions of the war, but we were not distracted from the goal we had set for ourselves.

Now that Dad was no longer with us, all the responsibilities of taking care of the family rested upon the shoulders of my mother and my sister. Mother was especially concerned about the safety of my sister who was now in her late teens. The Russian soldiers were known to mistreat and molest any girls they could find, knowing that they would suffer no consequences for their actions.

On one occasion, while we were in an area for more than a few weeks, we were put in a large two-story house with several other families. It was a country-like setting with a barn and a small field that had served as pasture for the animals that had at one time been there. Not far from the house was a good-sized crater where a bomb had exploded. It was obvious that this had been an area where the battle had left its marks, and it was not a safe place to be since the fighting was still very close. This house had an attic with a trap door on the second floor where odds and ends were stored, but now no one made use of it. It was not by choice that we stayed at this house for a longer period of time as it was, on a number of accounts, an insecure situation. The other occupants included several other families and their children, five or six of whom were teenage girls, my sister being one of them. There was always a concern for the girl's safety—especially when the Russian soldiers showed up—so the girls were told to be careful and stay out of sight as much as possible. They were also admonished to dress modestly and not use too much makeup so as not to needlessly attract attention to themselves.

For a while all was well until one of our neighbors, a lady who lived across the street, felt that she needed to score some points of favor from the soldiers. Not having to be concerned for herself as she was not exactly what the Russian soldiers were looking for in beauty, she maliciously informed the soldiers that there were six young girls staying in the house across the street. For this information, she would likely be rewarded with some special food that she otherwise would not be privileged to have. People sold each other out all too often for a pittance, small advantage or favor. We had to be ever vigilant, wary of everyone as we never knew whom we could trust. The girls had tried to stay out of sight when the soldiers were around, but most of them had found and freely applied makeup, which was not a good idea if the soldiers discovered them. My sister had taken the advice of some of the older ladies and dressed more simply. She had also refrained from having an overly fancy hairstyle and had applied no makeup. In order to appear less appealing to the soldiers, some girls even applied ashes to their faces to create an older, unhealthy effect.

After being informed that there were six young girls in our house, the soldiers wasted no time in checking things out for themselves. When the soldiers appeared in the yard, the girls frantically made their escape into the attic. They put a tall ladder up to the trap door that led to the attic, and once they were hidden away, some of the residents of the house removed the ladder and any evidence that might show where they were hiding. Roughly, the soldiers demanded entrance to our house declaring that they had been told that there were young girls in our house, and they demanded to see them. Since we were not forthcoming with information about whether there were girls living in our home, they stormed through searching the whole house. Their search proved to be fruitless, and they left very upset determined to deal with the lady that tipped them off. When confronted, the lady persistently told them that there were definitely six girls in that house, so they were back in short order to continue their search. They soon came to the realization that they had overlooked the attic. They proceeded to shoot at the ceiling causing the hapless girls to scream, thus giving up their cover. Instead of putting up a ladder for the girls to climb down, they ruthlessly demanded that they drop down from a height of about nine feet. At the bottom of the trap door were various kinds of garden tools and wooden trunks. Choosing to throw themselves down rather than be shot, some were badly hurt in the fall. My sister fared worse than the others and received severe injuries which actually saved her from being molested at that point. She was in bed for some time while recovering from her fall, which actually spared her from further abuse from the soldiers who came by unannounced day or night. The soldiers could not be bothered with an injured girl, so they took the others and went on their way. Appalling were some of the things that went on all around us. Sometimes we felt as if we were at our breaking point and could endure no more, but in our greatest fear and distress, God came to our rescue and we experienced His fatherly care.

> *Sometimes we felt as if we were at our breaking point and could endure no more, but in our greatest fear and distress, God came to our rescue and we experienced His fatherly care.*

My sister Erna, 18 years of age

It was sometime later when my sister had recovered from most of her injuries from the fall, when another soldier came calling. Watching his approach, my mother quickly told her to get into bed so she could say that she was not well. This was, of course, always true as long as we were under the control of communism and the appalling conditions that the war inflicted upon us. We were always in fear for our life and in great mental anguish from one day to the next. Despite his initial persistence that she should come with him, the soldier made the decision to leave my sister alone for the time being and come back when she had recovered. Our prayers went up for her to the only One that could help us, and He came through in a marvelous way. He inspired my sister in a unique course of action that not only saved her from the soldier's intentions, but also brought a blessing in its turn that we could never have imagined. The soldier came again and was now insistent that my sister should get out of bed and come with him. Sitting on the edge of her bed, he warned her that he did not believe that she was really that sick. Fearful and indignant, my sister told him that he should be ashamed of the thoughts he was having for her. She boldly told him that President Stalin loved children, and he would not tolerate such treatment from him. There actually was some truth to what she told him. Some of these communist leaders could be very brutal, but some had a soft heart for children and young people. When food was scarce and we had to resort to begging for food to stay alive, it was usually the children that were sent out. It was known among the refugees that people who had

> *After speaking to his conscience, my sister dauntlessly proceeded to give him a Bible study while he quietly sat on the bed. He was so affected by what he heard as he sat there listening intently to her words that when she was finished, he promised that he would treat her well in the future, and even protect her from any soldiers that would seek to harm her*

something to give found it harder to refuse young people than adults. After speaking to his conscience, my sister dauntlessly proceeded to give him a Bible study while he quietly sat on the bed. He was so affected by what he heard as he sat there listening intently to her words that when she was finished, he promised that he would treat her well in the future, and even protect her from any soldiers that would seek to harm her. The rest of the time that we remained at this house he came regularly to see if she was okay. This kind soldier did not come empty-handed, but brought us sugar, flour and other basic foods that were normally hard to come by. What an answer to prayer! How can people ever say, "There is no God"? He is definitely alive and He loves His children supremely, meeting their needs even before they call on Him.

The time had come for us to move on again. News had been received that those who had previously occupied or owned these properties were returning, and we would be driven out. Those who heeded these warnings knew it was better to move on voluntarily than to be forced out in haste and fury a day or two later. This seemed to be our new normal way of life where we would stay a short while in one place and then abruptly have to take whatever we could carry and move on. It was always our hope and prayer that our move would be ever closer in the direction of our escape route, just a little nearer toward the border where we could be free. Every place prepared us a bit more for the challenges that we would find at our next temporary place of abode. This continual moving from one place to the next had a clear effect on our outlook regarding the value of property. During these years we could never put our roots down too deeply anywhere. It was "here today and who knows where tomorrow." If we hadn't been aware before, living under these conditions taught us that each day has sufficient challenges of its own, and we would trust our heavenly Father to give us the strength needed to face whatever the next day would bring.

We were now in Poland, formerly controlled by the Russians, but at this point of the war it was under German occupation. The Germans had driven the Russians back, and had also driven many of the Polish people from their homes. These homes were now occupied by the German soldiers and German refugees. As you can imagine, this did not help to make good relations between us and the Polish people. We, of course, had no input in this decision. We were simply told where and when to go. Finding ourselves in the midst of fighting, we had little or no freedom to make decisions of our own. It didn't matter if we were under the control of the Russians or the Germans, rules were made or changed on short notice, and we had no choice but to fit in as best as we could. There were now a lot of uncertainties for even though we were right then under German occupation, the news was that the Russians were gaining strength, and that at any time the Germans would have to retreat. We knew that if that happened our conditions would be much worse, and it would be very difficult for us to make our escape to freedom.

The Germans, however, would not even consider defeat at this point, and assured everyone that they were winning the war and were there to stay. In order to strengthen their position, they sought to build up a spirit of nationalism. They introduced a law that all young people were to attend classes where they would be instructed to be true to the German Reich, with special emphasis on pledging allegiance to the Fuhrer, Adolph Hitler. By this time, Hitler did not have any respect for religious freedom. His only goal was to win the war and establish a world empire. The classes that the youth were to attend were compulsory. Only a severe illness could excuse any youth from attending, provided they had a signed letter from a physician stating clearly why this person was unable to attend the Hitler Youth classes. In these classes they were instructed that their full allegiance was always to be to Hitler, the Fuhrer. We were told that if any parent did not support this program, they would be severely dealt with and their children would be taken from them and become wards of the state. My sister Erna was of the age that she was required to attend, but it was obvious to her and our whole family that it would interfere with our commitment to God, and He must have first claims on our life above that of Hitler and his philosophy. Yet, if we did not comply, the consequences could be devastating. Erna could be taken from our family.

We now turned to the only Source of help we knew, the One who had never failed us no matter how distressing our situation appeared to be. Like Daniel's friends, our resolve was, *"our God whom we serve is able to deliver us" (Dan. 3:17).* Whoever or whatever the circumstances, we would put our full trust in Him, come what may.

A short while before Erna had to show up for the Hitler Youth meetings, she noticed two small sores on one of her legs that were quite painful. These sores quickly turned into large, ulcer-like sores that ate into the flesh—right to the bone. The pain was unbearable and she was not able to walk. The doctor was called, but he was unable to successfully alleviate the condition. The infection became so severe that he considered amputation might be necessary in order to save my sister's life. In the meantime, he ordered strict bed rest. She was not permitted to put any weight on her leg in the hope that it might bring relief. In the days that followed she was

Chapter 5 Protection in Crisis 67

confined to her bed with compresses on the affected parts of her leg, but instead of getting better, each day it grew worse. As the time drew nearer to the day that Erna was to show up for her Hitler Youth meetings, the doctor gave her a letter stating that he had ordered strict bed rest for her since her condition had become increasingly worse with each passing day. We also continued to pray that the Lord would prevent the need for amputation.

On the first day of the Hitler Youth meetings Erna was not present. When Erna did not show up a German police officer came to our house to see her the very next day. The officer was not persuaded that her infection was as serious as we stated, but after seeing the letter from the doctor, he reluctantly accepted her absence, but assured us that he would be back to check on her the following week. He admonished that we should not think that this would be a lasting reason to excuse her from attending these important classes.

And now, suddenly and without warning, the news came that the Russians were making great advances in driving the Germans back out of Poland. We were told that within days we could expect to be under Russian control again. This news brought with it new anxieties. What would happen to us and, in particular, how could we be on the move again, walking many miles, when Erna was to have strict bed rest? Now we witnessed another miracle. The deep sores that were so severely infected as to have the doctor consider amputation, gradually began to heal and

> *On the first day of the Hitler Youth meetings Erna was not present. When Erna did not show up a German police officer came to our house to see her the very next day. The officer was not persuaded that her infection was as serious as we stated, but after seeing the letter from the doctor, he reluctantly accepted her absence, but assured us that he would be back to check on her the following week.*

dry up. The doctor could not believe his eyes. The infection had lasted for many weeks providing a plausible excuse for my sister not to attend a single Hitler Youth meeting.

When the Russians arrived, they came so swiftly that the German troops were not prepared for them. The Russian's first focus was on the youth who had attended the Hitler Youth meetings where they were programmed to give first allegiance to Hitler, and the winning of the war for Germany. They were now considered to be the greatest enemies of the Russians. They immediately rounded up all the Hitler Youth and made arrangements to send them on a train to Siberia. Since my sister was not among that group, she was saved from being separated from us. This news of the young people being sent to Siberia spread quickly all over Europe and my father, who was still absent and searching for us, also heard of it and was afraid that he would never see his daughter again, as he feared that she too had been sent to Siberia.

My sister's leg healed just in time for us to continue on our pilgrimage as refugees. God had again come to our rescue in a way we could not have anticipated. Erna's scars remain as a reminder to all of us of the marvelous way God answered our prayers on her behalf. Unbeknownst to us at the time, we would soon be reunited with our father. This desire and our intent to escape to freedom gave us hope to continue on until our plans would become a reality. During these difficult years we never gave up hope, and neither did my father. Our faith in God kept us from giving up when thousands around us did. We put our trust in the promise of Deuteronomy 31:8, *"And the LORD, he it is that doth go before thee; he will be with thee, he will not fail thee, neither forsake thee: fear not, neither be dismayed."*

Chapter 6
Family Reunion

Many atrocities were inflicted on the civilians during World War II. One of the most uncompassionate acts was the separation of thousands of families with but a few of these families being reunited until some time had passed after the war had ended. It was all too common for the men to be taken and forced into battle to help their side win and end the war. This would usually be where the fighting was at its fiercest so that few survived the ordeal. When the fighting finally ceased and peace was declared, thousands upon thousands of men had lost their lives, leaving the burden of leading and supporting the family households to the women. A family was usually considered to consist of a mother and her children. Men who were not fighting were forced to work in factories that produced more trucks, jeeps, tanks and ammunition to replenish the stocks that were quickly diminished as the intense fighting continued. Others were sent to concentration camps, or Siberia, or shot at the cruel whim of the communist leaders who were in charge of their destiny. Life was indeed very cheap.

The women were usually sent to work in the factories, or in large fields where they cultivated and harvested crops such as potatoes, turnips and sugar beets. The young girls were assigned to work in large kitchens where the soldiers were fed. At times, this was also where some of the thousands of refugees who flooded the area received food.

Travel during the war was difficult. If you needed transportation, it would be whatever you could afford or find at the time. Passenger trains, if available, were primarily used to transport soldiers to and from the battlefields. Closed cattle trains were also used for the same purpose. Open train cars were used to transport war equipment, and many times desperate refugees who had lost everything were consigned to this method of travel. Some of the refugees were sent to larger centers where they could be better accommodated, but many, especially the German people who were considered to be the enemy, were sent to the frightful concentration camps or the dreaded Siberia. Other methods of travel were whatever you could find at the time.

We once started out hopefully with a wagon that was pulled by an ox. When the soldiers saw it, however, they relieved us of the wagon and most the contents as we were not able to remove them quickly enough. Whoever had the greatest authority would end up with the best mode of travel. It was the survival of the fittest that ruled the day. Basically, most people had to walk either willingly, or were mercilessly forced to keep pace by the soldiers.

Great uncertainty about the future loomed over the people. The nations of Europe were not secure. Some of the largest cities of Europe, Berlin included, were reduced to ashes, twisted steel and rubble. France had surrendered to the Nazis. Thousands had lost their homes, their possessions, everything they had diligently worked for all their lives. The area was inundated with the homeless and refugees, and in this mass of confusion they searched for family members who had become separated from them. In some cases, the Russian soldiers ordered the refugees to board trains, promising them that they were being sent back to their homes. In reality, these trains were headed for Siberia. When the trains were heavily loaded with people and would not hold any more, they would leave the station regardless of the fact that some family members were on the train while other members of the same family were not successful in getting on board before it reached its capacity and left the station, leaving them behind. That is how many families were torn apart. Quite often, refugees were forced onto large army trucks and shipped off to concentration camps. There was no merciful attempt to keep members of the same family together. In the confusion generated by the war, many families lost one or more of their beloved family members, never to be united again.

Our family experienced the same fate twice. When we were separated from our father the first time in the early years of the war for six months, we had no idea where he had been taken, whether he was dead or alive, or whether we would ever see him again. The second time when we were separated for one year and three months, we did not know where he was, nor did he know where to look for us. Before he was suddenly taken from us, we had a family council meeting where we discussed what our strategy should be if we would ever be separated again. We promised that we would endeavor to find each other while still in communist territory, and then together make our escape to the West. From West Germany, we would then immigrate to Canada where our father's mother had immigrated in 1925. However, since conditions for German people in communist controlled countries grew increasingly worse toward the end of the war, we decided that after a time of unsuccessfully searching for each other in the East, we would engage in a different plan. It was agreed that our father, wherever he might be, and Mother and the rest of us, wherever the conditions of war would bring us, would try to secretly cross the border to West Germany. There, in a country of freedom, we would resume our efforts to find each other.

It was now time for us to implement our plan. One year and three months was a long time to be separated from each other, and difficult questions needed to be resolved. Where should we look for our father? Was he drafted in the army? Was he a prisoner of war? Was he sent to Siberia? Or worse yet, was he killed in the war?

> *While we were each speculating where the missing members of our family might be and how we could be reunited, it was extraordinary how God worked in our lives to bring this about.*

These and many other questions about our father's whereabouts filled our minds as we set out to find him.

Father had similar thoughts. Where could his family be? There were reports circulating that numerous women and children had been sent farther east, and many even to Siberia. Other reports indicated that many had been sent to larger cities and housed in empty factories or large warehouses.

While we were each speculating where the missing members of our family might be and how we could be reunited, it was extraordinary how God worked in our lives to bring this about. I will now share my father's experience in his effort to find us. The war was now over, but the conditions in the East were wholly unsound. As Germans, we were completely without rights or privileges in the land as we were considered to be the people who were responsible for the war and all its misery. We were now the aim of people's revenge making it even more difficult for German refugees to find lost family members.

In the meantime, Father was assigned to work as a prisoner of war at a factory that produced all manner of fruit jams and chocolates. The factory was located very close to Berlin and the border where we intended to cross into freedom. We would later recognize God's leading in this as it would make it easier for us to escape to the West. Should our father be able to find us and bring us to where he was, we would all have a better chance to make our way to freedom as a reunited family.

God answered my father's prayers in a way that he could never have imagined. Since religious freedom did not exist in communism, he might again be faced with Sabbath problems. Working on Sabbath was not an option that he ever considered, but there was always the fear of the consequences. Imagine the joy and thankfulness in his heart when he learned that the factory owner, his boss, was a Seventh-day Adventist who also kept the Sabbath. God is so good. He sees the end from the beginning and often answers our prayers before we even ask. For now, he had religious freedom and could keep the Sabbath as was his custom. Yet the blessings did not stop. While there were people everywhere who were starving, my father was now working where he had the kind of food that had grown in the Garden of Eden. There was all manner of dried fruits that he would be working with and, more importantly, had permission to freely eat.

My father's new workplace consisted of a compound the size of a small farm and was located a few miles from the nearest village. In this compound, there was a large building that had previously been an ammunitions factory. There were also several houses used by some of the factory workers and one of these was reserved for us if and when my father found us. The compound was enclosed by a high wooden fence. The large gate at the main entrance as well as a smaller gate were locked after business hours. This was in East Germany, yet it was controlled by the communists since the war had ended, and security was strictly adhered to. The factory owner was German and since this was still German territory, he was the rightful owner of the property. When the communists took over, however, he had to give an account of everything he was doing. The communists would now frequently appear at the factory and if they spied something on the property that they desired, they would help themselves to it. The owner was helpless to prevent this thievery. Being a prudent businessman, however, the factory owner had anticipated this before communism took over that part of the country. In order to avoid major losses, he had dug large pits and buried many barrels of raw product in the ground behind his factory. There were countless barrels of dried figs, raisins, apricots, apples, pears and other dried fruits which were used to make a variety of jams. He produced a large variety of chocolates and also had an assortment of nuts.

It was not long before my father was placed in charge of the buildings and grounds as the manager and he was privy to the location of all of these products. It was his responsibility to dig up the supplies as they were needed in the factory, but this had to be done at a time when no one else was around. Though the war was over in East Germany, one could never know who you could trust. It was because of this that the factory owner was relieved to know that my father was a Christian and someone he could put his full confidence and trust in. He gave him the keys to the whole property and entrusted him with his entire business.

There was no peace of mind for my father, however, while he was still missing his family. He knew that he must make a strong effort to find us. He made inquiries wherever possible as to where most of the women and children had been sent. He was told that there were many refugees in several parts of the country where he could start to look for his family. But how could he know where to start? It was like finding a needle in a haystack. Another person told him that they were quite certain that women and children had recently been loaded on train cars and sent to Siberia. Yet another report was that the Russians had killed numerous women and children when they attempted to escape. With all these conflicting reports, my father did not know what to think or where to look first. His employer was very sympathetic, but he valued him as a worker and did not want to lose him.

The news from all sides was very discouraging, and he realized there was only one Source he could rely on. God had never failed him in the past, bringing him through many seemingly impossible situations. For several days he fasted and prayed earnestly that God would give him the wisdom to know how to proceed. He also prayed that his employer would be willing to give him some time off from work that would enable him to fully concentrate on his search for his family. One day stretched into another, until one day my father was gratified to hear his employer say to him, "I see that you are so sad about the loss of your family. If you have a clue where you might find them, I will give you some time from work, as long as you promise me that once you have found them, you will return to me and not leave me."

One evening after work, my father again earnestly prayed that the Lord would help him find his family. Tired from the duties of the day, he decided to retire for the night hopeful that the Lord would direct him on how to proceed after being refreshed from a good night's rest. Sometimes things may look dark and discouraging in the evening, but the morning has a tendency to bring with it a little sunshine. Exhausted, he soon fell into a deep sleep. As he slept, he had a very interesting dream. He dreamt that he was in the midst of a crowd of people who were all going in the same direction and since he was in amongst this jostling crowd, he had no choice but to go in the same direction. Presently he asked, "Where is everyone going?" The answer came back, "We're going home." He thought that was a great idea; home is where he also wanted to go to be with his family, so he continued along with the crowd taking him where everyone else was going.

As the dream continued, they all came to a train station. There stood a long train and everyone boarded this train without hesitation. There were so many people to board the train that there was scarcely room for them all. Packed like sardines in a can, some sat and many more stood occupying every small bit of space. Before boarding the train, my father glanced around and saw a freight train on the other side of the tracks. He took particular note of the location and color of some of the train cars. Blowing a warning whistle, the train slowly gained momentum as everyone rejoicingly exclaimed, "We are going home!" He noticed that the countryside was somehow still quite beautiful as the train chugged along leaving behind one village after another. After a few hours the train came to a stop near a small village. Everyone got off the train. My father asked, "Where are we?" "Why are we stopping here?" The people answered, "The train is just making a brief stop so that everyone can get off and take a little rest, and then we will continue on our way." My father joined the others and stretched his legs after the crowded, two-hour ride. He observed the surroundings of that small train station and took note of the buildings and another train on a second track. He didn't see anything that was familiar about this place. He noticed that one end of the railroad station had been bombed and had sustained major damage. Part of the roof was gone and some of the walls were reduced to a pile of bricks. With that, the dream ended and my father awoke wondering what it all meant.

The night was still young as my father lay there thinking about going home. How he wished it was a reality rather than a mere dream! It was a very dark night, but my father had a luminous watch that illuminated the time, and he noted that it was well past midnight. Very tired and thankful that it was not yet time to get up, he once again fell back into a deep slumber. A short time later he awoke with a start. He looked at his watch and realized that he had scarcely slept fifteen minutes, but he had once again had a dream. Strangely, it was the same dream that he had experienced but a short fifteen minutes ago. Now he was wide awake and sleep was the furthest thing from his mind. Why would he dream the same dream twice? What was the meaning of all of this? Then he remembered that someone else had the same experience in Bible times. Pharaoh had dreamt a similar dream twice, and when Joseph was asked to interpret the dreams, he said to Pharaoh, *"And for that the dream was doubled unto Pharaoh twice; it is because the thing is established by God, and God will shortly bring it to pass" (Gen. 41:32).* This was too good to be true. Could it be that God had answered his prayers and

The night was still young as my father lay there thinking about going home. How he wished it was a reality rather than a mere dream!

that he would soon be reunited with his family? Now morning could not come soon enough. The first thing he would do was tell his employer that he must set out at once to find his family whom he had not seen for over a year. His faith was now strengthened, and he did not have a moment to lose.

Morning finally came, and as he excitedly shared his dreams with his boss, he also was convinced that this was a direct intervention of the Lord. He agreed to give my father a few days off from work to find his family, but only with the assurance that he would return as soon as he had found them. My father agreed, and within a short time he was on his way. He would follow the journey shown to him in the dream and find his family. That should not be very complicated, but as he left the house the realization hit him that in his dream he was not told where he would find his family. He saw only that all the people in his dream were supposedly going home. How would he know where to start his journey? Unsure of where to go, he decided to just start walking to the nearest town in the hope that something familiar would reveal itself—and it surely did! He soon found himself in the midst of a lot of people, German soldiers and civilians alike. As he inquired where they were all headed, the reply was, "We are going to freedom, and we are going home." That was good news. If that part of the dream had come to pass, the rest would surely become reality as well.

In a short while everyone arrived at the train station—the same station my father had seen in his dream. The surroundings were an exact replica of what my father had seen in his dream, and he could now scarcely contain the joy that swelled within his heart. He was actually going home. He would soon find his family. He did not have all the answers yet as to how and when, but so far everything was as he was shown in his dream. The shrill sound of the train's whistle beckoned everyone aboard indicating that the train would leave the station momentarily. As the train pulled away from the station, great anticipation filled the hearts of everyone aboard at the thought that their greatest hopes would soon become reality.

Let me now take you back some weeks before the dream and the actual journey on the train. My father's first attempt to find his family was made by mail. During the war there was practically no mail service as most post offices had been destroyed and lay among the ruins of the communities they had served. In some cases, the Red Cross served as an emergency mail service whenever the fighting of the war lessened in certain areas. People would then write to the Red Cross inquiring if they had any information about a particular person or family. If by chance that family or person had also written to the Red Cross, they would put both letters together and send them to one of the inquiring parties. This would give them the information they needed to find each other. There was great rejoicing when people found each other through this method, and it usually became the talk of the town. It also served to encourage others who were also searching for their loved ones to not give in to discouragement and give up too soon. My father, in his search for his family, was told by some that a number of refugees had been taken to a certain area near a small village, and he might find his family there. On doing further study on the name of that village, however, he discovered that there were several villages by that same name. In which area should he now look? Sometimes he received conflicting reports from people who thought they had an idea where his family was, but later found these reports to be untrustworthy.

Since the war was over, the mail now began to be more or less regulated again. My father followed the agreement that he and Mother had made in the event that they should ever be separated during the war. He would send a letter to our church headquarters in Berlin, hoping that my mother was able to do the same. When both letters eventually arrived in Berlin, they would be put together and then mailed to either him or to my mother. In this way, one or the other would know where the other members of the family were located and could then proceed with a plan to find them. My father had previously, on several occasions, sent a letter to Berlin to find us, but there had been no response. He had to assume that his letters had gotten lost, or that my mother's letters had not arrived there to make a connection. Neither he nor we were to know what actually happened until much later. Our prayers were being answered from both sides, but we would not know that until it actually happened.

A few weeks before my father started out on his journey to find his family, he gathered as much available verbal information as possible from some of the other German refugees in the area. The word was out that many women with their children had been forced to flee westward, and it was possible that his family could be among them. During the German occupation of Poland, many fled from their homes. The German refugees eventually moved into these empty houses. When the war came to an end, the communists drove the German soldiers out of Poland, and with them many of the German refugees were driven further west to East Germany.

Thus it was that Father now decided to write a letter addressed to my mother, in care of our church headquarters' office in Berlin. In the event that my mother would do the same, he would discover our location and would know where he must travel on the train to find us. Unbeknownst to him at the time, this is exactly what happened. As he would later learn, his letter arrived in Berlin in the morning, and since they did not have a letter from us inquiring about him, they temporarily set his letter aside. My sister had also written to Berlin inquiring about the whereabouts of my father. Her letter arrived there in the afternoon of the same day. Realizing that both letters belonged together, they opted to readdress my sister's letter to my father putting his letter in with hers and sent both to him. When my father received the letters, he was greatly relieved to know that we were still alive near a town called Kamin. He now had our address. He immediately sat down and wrote a letter to us saying that he was coming soon to find us and take us back to his workplace. His feelings of relief and joy now that he knew where to find us were somewhat tempered, however, when he inquired about the whereabouts of this town. He learned, to his dismay, that there were several towns by a similar name in East Germany. Now he was unsure at which town named Kamin he would find us. He didn't know where he needed to leave the train, he just knew that he must follow his dream.

Although the train was overly crowded with most people standing or sitting on their backpacks, the lack of comfort was not now considered to be a hardship. Any inconveniences that might have to be endured along the way would be well worth the anticipated reward of arriving home at the end of the day. Time passed quickly and several hours had gone past before most realized it. As the train slowly came to a stop near a little village, it was all in harmony with his dream. Everyone listened closely as an announcement was made indicating that the train would stop here for a short time to drop off packages and letters for that area and take on supplies before continuing on further. Most got off the train to stretch tired limbs or go for a short walk around the station, and my father decided to do the same. As he got off the train and scanned the yard, he noticed the second train on the sidetrack appeared just as he had seen it in his dream. Moreover, some of the freight cars of the train on the second track were red just as in his dream and in the exact location as he had seen them. Making his way to the train station, he recognized it from his dream, although he had never traveled in this part of the world before.

It was now almost time to re-board the train to continue the journey. My father quickly realized that everything in his dream had been fulfilled so far, but this is when his dream came to an end. What was he to do now? He was not told in the dream what would happen next. Should he board the train and continue his journey and, if so, how much farther must he go to find his family? The train was about to pull out of the station, and my father had to decide whether or not to board the train. It is amazing how the Lord answers our prayers when we trust Him and submit totally to His leading. As my father anxiously contemplated what he should do, the Lord performed another miracle.

Although the name of this little town was the same name that appeared on my sister's letter that he had received, there was another village by the same name further on, possibly in a different county. As my father wondered what he must do next, he witnessed a mail delivery right there at this small train station. People from the little village had come to the train station to receive their mail. The mailman had climbed on top of a wagon that was normally used to transport parcels from the station onto the train. Taking one letter after another he shouted the last name of the person the letter was addressed to, and if that person was present, they would move forward to receive their mail. There were those who had not received any letters for a long time, and becoming discouraged, would not show up for the daily mail delivery. If that happened and a letter did arrive for them, usually one of their neighbors would receive it and deliver it to them, provided the mailman knew them and approved.

My father heard the mailman shout out one name after another, and suddenly, hardly believing what he was hearing, the mailman shouted out the name, "Hiebert! Hiebert!" as he waved yet another letter over his head. He at once left the train and made his way to the wagon where the mailman stood and replied, "Here, I'm here. That letter is for me." The mailman looked at my father and said, "No, this letter is not for you. It is for a widow with three children." My father responded, "I think that's the widow I'm looking for." The letter that the mailman had was the very letter that my father had sent to us after he had received the two letters from Berlin. My sister and mother had made several attempts to find my father without success, therefore, they did not show up to pick up the mail this particular day. My father's train had stopped there and paused just long enough for my father to witness the mail delivery that morning. My father was not aware that his letter addressed to us was on the same train as he was. When the mailman gave my father the letter, it was the one he had written to us to tell us when he would come for us. Incredibly, it was my father that ended up helping the mail service deliver his own letter. The Lord's timing is amazing. It was his own letter that helped identify where he needed to get off the train to find us. I don't remember whether he even read the letter to us, for from here on he could tell us everything in person. What a reunion that was!

> *On hearing the news of his arrival, my sister ran down the lane from the house where we were staying and was the first to greet him. Mother and the rest of us followed as quickly as our feet would take us. From a distance my mother recognized him, and with inexpressible joy in her heart said, "That's my David."*

I am sure it was no coincidence that there were some folk at the train station to receive their mail who lived in the same house where we were. Witnessing the exchange between my father and the mailman, they immediately ran home eager to share such rare good news with my family. They told us that a tall man who was at the train station was looking for his family. On hearing the news of his arrival, my sister ran down the lane from the house where we were staying and was the first to greet him. Mother and the rest of us followed as quickly as our feet would take us. From a distance my mother recognized him, and with inexpressible joy in her heart said, "That's my David." In some of Mother's romantic moments, during the many months she was separated from my father, she would imagine how it would be to be reunited again someday with the love of her life. She pictured herself walking down a lovely lane with graceful trees on either side in a beautiful country setting; there to meet, never to part again. The Lord granted her wish even to the last detail. What a homecoming!

Food had been rather scarce and very simple at the place where my father found us. Anticipating this, he had brought with him a large backpack filled with all manner of dried fruits—figs, apricots, apples, pears, raisins and even some delicious chocolates from the factory where he worked. The people who lived in the same building where we were rejoiced with mixed emotions that we had found each other. They were so pleased for us yet at the same time were sad that they had not been reunited with their loved ones. An experience like ours was rare, and when it occurred it was the news of the community. After four days we were on our way to where my father lived and worked, but we were now more determined than ever to escape across the border to West Germany as soon as it could be arranged.

Though we may not comprehend at the time all the aspects of His design, our heavenly Father has a master plan for each of us. We were intensely grateful when, through God's miraculous leading, we were brought together as a family just months before we had to make the most dangerous decision of all—to cross the East German border into West Germany. This was the time when we most needed Dad's strong faith and guiding leadership. Until one's endurance is put to the test, it is impossible to know what one is capable of living through. The war years forced us into situations that we could not possibly have prepared for, and without a strong faith in God we would not have survived the torment that surrounded us. In those dark days when many around us had lost all faith in man and God, we placed our trust in the only One who was able to bring us through the raging storms that threatened to destroy us. We often repeated and clung to Bible promises such as *"God is our refuge and strength, a very present help in trouble. The LORD of hosts is with us; the God of Jacob is our refuge"* (Ps. 46:1, 7).

Chapter 7
Crossing the Swamp

As the Second World War was nearing its close, it became evident that once powerful nations that had held leading positions in the world were now defeated. They were now dominated by the victors of the war, and these conquerors wasted no time in expressing their newly established authority. For the sake of survival, those of us who were victims of the war—now mostly refugees—had to recognize the new order of power and to whom allegiance was now due.

As the conquering power, the Soviet Union was now the power to be reckoned with. The Russians had driven the Germans back out of their country and were now in control of the eastern part of Germany, including the capital, East Berlin. As the defeated enemy, all refugees and prisoners of war were required to work for the Russian conquerors. The non-negotiable conditions of employment were that we were to work without monetary remuneration and, at best, be provided with a bit of food that fell far short of enough to feed a family. Those who worked were able to eat sparingly. A third of a loaf of bread might be their pay for a day's work, and those that were too young or too sick to work had to do without. The hours were usually long and overtaxing. Rather than an employee/employer relationship, it was a servant/master relationship. You did your utmost to please your taskmaster so that your life and that of your family might be spared. Life was not respected but considered very cheap in the eyes of our enemies. Many lives were lost, and many more were sent to

Siberia where they were seldom heard from again. Some of my extended family were sent to Siberia, and only God knows what happened to them.

A particular experience that took place in the part of the Iron Curtain where we then resided details well the controlling power that man is capable of wielding over his fellow man when their status is reversed. A man known to my father, whom we will call Manfried, was assigned to work in a factory a few kilometers from where he and his family resided in a tiny cabin. He was expected to work long hours and show up for work very early. He knew that if he arrived late for work, he would suffer serious consequences, perhaps to the extent that his family might never hear from him again. Being late for work or not showing up at all, therefore, was never considered to be a wise option. Manfried was always punctual, for his own sake as well as for the sake of his family. One morning, however, time had slipped by much faster than he realized, and he knew that he would not be able to make it to work at the designated time. He shuddered at the thought of facing the consequences that would surely be forced upon him. Desperate, knowing that he must not be late at any cost, a thought that could solve his problem, and possibly even his life, came to his mind.

Between his humble little cabin and the factory where Manfried worked was a large swamp. It was discovered that if a direct route was made over the swamp from the area where Manfried lived, the time required to arrive at the factory for work would be cut in half. Over the course of time, a number of men from Manfried's village undertook to build a simple boardwalk over the swamp. Material was scarce, but in due course some posts and planks were found for the job. The men worked as time permitted. Posts were pounded into the swamp five or six feet apart, and planks of about six inches in width were nailed securely to the top of the posts to cover the full length of the swamp, which was several hundred feet.

Using the boardwalk to cross the swamp would save much valuable time, and this particular morning Manfried needed a miracle. Great care needed to be taken in order to keep one's balance, however, since the planks over the swamp were very narrow. If one tried to cross in haste, it was almost inevitable that you would fall into the swamp which housed various sea weeds, frogs, water and plenty of mud and slime. It was for this reason that the swamp boardwalk was usually left as a last resort. There was also an unwritten but well understood rule by those who frequented this shortcut that before crossing you must first check to see if someone had already started over the boardwalk from the other side. The one that reached the middle first had the right to complete the crossing. This meant that the other person had to turn around and retrace his steps, giving way to the person that had entered first.

Manfried realized that there was no other option, and he didn't have a minute to lose. He quickly checked to see if anyone had started on the boardwalk from the opposing side. Since all was clear, he hurried as fast as he could without losing his balance on the narrow planks. He was almost to the middle of the boardwalk when he noticed, to his great dismay, that someone was starting onto the boardwalk from the other side. It was still early in the morning and a bit dark so he could not tell at first who this individual was. He could only make out the form of a man. As Manfried glanced up to see if the person who had started across the boardwalk had observed the unspoken rule and had turned back, he noted that he himself was well past the middle of the distance of the boardwalk that covered the swamp. Then, as he approached closer to this stranger, he was horrified to see that the man coming toward him was a Russian army officer in full uniform and decorated with many distinguishing medals. It was obvious that the officer had no intention of going back. The officer knew that all assigned workers at the factory had to appear for work at the time specified and may very well have had a part to play in deciding what the consequences would be if the workers failed to meet these demands. Yet, he had no regard for Manfried or what might happen to him if he arrived late for work.

Manfried did not have many options. If he continued forward, either he or the officer would most likely end up in the swamp. If it ended up being the officer, Manfried would almost surely face serious consequences as the officer would certainly hold him responsible for his misfortune. The officer used his position and rank as authority to order Manfried to give him his due honor and preference. Manfried, however, was in a no-win situation. If he yielded to the officer, he would be late for work, and he would have to answer to his factory supervisor and face the consequences for not showing up for work on time. In fact, if he were to end up in the swamp, he would be in such a mess that it would require a bath and complete change of clothing before he could even think of going to work. That would be much worse than being a few minutes late.

He had to make a quick decision and live with the consequences. It's amazing what can happen in just a few seconds. As the two approached each other on the narrow planks, the one that could keep his balance would be the one to be able to continue with that morning's appointments. The severe punishment for not showing up for work outweighed the challenges

of what the officer might do to him later—that is, if the officer could identify and find him. Manfried did make it to his place of work in time, but
in the process of passing each other, the officer ended up in the swamp.
Needless to say, the officer was not impressed that Manfried had refused
to retrace his steps and go back the way he had come. Manfried could only
hope that the officer would not find him after he was done cleaning his
uniform, or ever discover his identity. For now, he had made it to work on
time, and he would later deal with whatever came his way. During these
times, those who had no religious principles lived moment by moment,
trusting in their own wisdom in making the decisions that would serve
them best for the situation they were confronted with at the time.

That day seemed to be unusually long for Manfried. He tried to concentrate on his work while at the same time anxiously considering what
might be facing him if the officer caught up with him. It seemed that the
officer needed most of the day to clean himself up from his unfortunate
ordeal of the morning, and Manfried was able to work until evening without encountering a visit from him. Would the officer be watching for him
as he left the factory, and follow him to his home? Should he and his
family immediately engage on a plan of escape? What if he did not have
time enough to escape before the officer discovered where he lived? What
would happen to his family if his escape plan did not work out? These and
many other questions disturbed his mind all through the day. Finally, his
long day at work came to an end, and Manfried went on his way home to
share his ordeal with his family. All along the way he nervously kept looking over his shoulder to see if he was being followed, or for anything that
seemed suspiciously out of the ordinary. When he reached his home, he
breathed a sigh of relief. For now, at least, he was safe and would soon be
in the company of those he loved. Tomorrow would be another day when
he would have time to reflect on what his options were, and what might be
the most advisable course of action to avoid further problems. Uppermost
in his mind was the safety of his family, and upon his arrival at home he
sought their input in the development of a plan for their future.

Since he had not been followed on his way home, Manfried felt somewhat safe for now. After greeting his wife and children, he shared with
them the events of the day. They listened in shocked disbelief but agreed
with him that they should wait a little longer to engage on a plan to escape
from this area. Their hope was that the officer would not know where to
look for them, while knowing there was a very slim chance of that. For
now, they felt that there was nothing more that could be done to change
the situation. The day had been extremely stressful, and a good night's

rest could prove to give them a clearer perspective on their problems and a solution for the challenges that faced them.

Manfried and his family lived in a tiny cabin that had been deserted by the former owners. They had barely escaped with their lives when the fierce fighting of World War II found its way into that area. When the battle shifted to other regions, any homes that had not been utterly bombed and destroyed were soon occupied by the refugees that had survived the ordeal. No one owned anything at that time. It was the same with our family. Sometimes we were forced to move because of the fighting, and other times the Russians would drive us out and move their soldiers in. We lived in many places during the years of that terrible war. From one day to the next, we did not know where we would find rest at the end of the day.

Manfried's home was small but served his needs during that time. This home had no basement. There was only a cellar with a dirt floor. These cellars were usually quite cool because of the earthen floor and, therefore, were used to keep food cool since there was no refrigeration available. Stores did not sell vegetables in the winter and if they did, no one had any money to buy them. Manfried's wife, however, managed to secure a barrel which she filled with as many pickles as she could obtain. At the far end of the kitchen, and to the side of the main entrance of the cabin, was a sizable trap door with a ladder going straight down into the cellar. At the bottom was the barrel with the pickles. The family was accustomed to dining on a very meager diet and the pickles were usually their only source of vegetables. Food was scarce, but the source of strength for their existence was their close family ties. After the evening meal, the family retired in the hope that the next day would offer a solution that would keep them safe.

The next morning Manfried made sure that he had plenty of time to be at his place of work. He chose a different route to go to the factory and made sure he was not followed. All went well, and he arrived for work safely, and the rest of the day went well. Manfried knew, however, that he could never let his guard down. In those times, no one ever felt totally safe, day or night. When he returned from work that evening, the family again sat down to a meager meal, and pickles were again part of the menu. One of the children had been asked to open the big trap door and bring up enough pickles from the barrel for the evening meal, but in the haste of helping to prepare for the evening meal, they forgot to close the trap door.

The family was enjoying the meal and each other's company when suddenly there was a loud knock on the cabin door. Fearing who might be there at this time of the evening, Manfried decided that it would be best if he would answer the door. His greatest fear was realized when he opened the door and saw the army officer before him with his newly cleaned uniform and all his brightly shining medals polished to perfection. The officer had done some research to find the man that he had encountered while trying to cross the swamp. Now he had come to show his authority and mete out the punishment that he felt was necessary to reestablish the power that he had over Manfried. He had no interest to hear why Manfried was in such a hurry the morning before.

> *After desperately pleading for his life and promising not to bother Manfried and his family anymore, the officer was assisted out of the pickle barrel and on his way home smelling like a pickle. Within two days he had the opportunity of cleaning his uniform twice; once from the mud and grime of the swamp and the second time from the smell of the pickle juice.*

It's amazing how fast one can assess a dangerous situation and come up with a plan to save one's life, and the lives of your loved ones. Manfried's plan had to be good, and he did not have a minute to lose. Instantly, he realized that he could quickly turn a life-threatening experience in his favor and save himself and his family. As the officer came farther into the room to confront him, Manfried hastily took two large steps towards the officer and shouted, "What! Do you dare to come into my home and threaten me and my family?!" This was a response that the officer was totally unprepared for as he considered that he was in control of what was to transpire next. When Manfried took the two large steps toward him, the officer's automatic response was to take two large steps backwards, which took him right into the open trap door. Before he had time to react, he fell through the trap door and into the pickle barrel in the cellar below. It occurred so fast that it was all over before one could really grasp what happened. In a flash Manfried closed the trap door to remove any way of escape for the now desperate army officer who was now at Manfried's mercy. In just a few seconds the scene had changed completely. Now, fancy uniform and high-ranking medals were of no use.

After desperately pleading for his life and promising not to bother Manfried and his family anymore, the officer was assisted out of the pickle barrel and on his way home smelling like a pickle. Within two days he had the opportunity of cleaning his uniform twice; once from the mud and grime of the swamp and the second time from the smell of the pickle juice.

The war was at its close now, and Manfried's family moved to the West in the event that the officer might change his mind and come back in retaliation. However, this was the last encounter he had with this officer, never hearing from him again. The officer may also have learned a most valuable lesson; that all people should be treated kindly and with respect regardless of rank or position. As we lived through the terrible years of the war and often in the midst of it, we discovered that there were still soldiers with a heart for the sufferings of humanity on both sides of the war. Some of these soldiers may have even been angels in human form sent to protect us from greater danger or supply us with food when in our greatest need.

Chapter 8

Escape to Freedom

It was the spring of 1946 when we finally arrived at my father's place of work in the northern part of East Germany. The gray of winter had passed and now in mid-March there were the beginning signs of nature's reawakening. The budding cherry trees promised beauty amidst the ravaged countryside. Politically, the Second World War had come to an end the year before, but we were by no means free to do as we pleased. Communism was in control and still greatly affected our work, worship and livelihood. The fighting had ceased, but there remained much uncertainty in the land. We now had a more permanent place to live as long as we stayed where my father worked, but even that could quickly change if the Russians interfered in his business and banished him elsewhere—which they were very capable of doing. The Russians sent many families back to their original homes after the war was over. That would have been very unsettling for us since the enemy had burned our house shortly after we left the area in the Ukraine. We would not have had a home to go back to, and we had no idea where they might send us. Our German heritage was not looked upon with favor as we were still considered to be the people that first caused the war and all its miseries. We were fortunate in that as long as we were able to stay where we were for now, my father's employment relationship with his employer was excellent. In fact, he pled with my father to stay with him and not flee to West Germany. Because my father was a Christian, as was his employer, he felt he could trust him with his entire business. He told him, "You are like an angel that God sent to me at just the time when I needed you most."

During this time of apparent calm, we were able to live according to the dictates of our conscience and worship on Sabbath without fear of retribution. My father was a born leader and worked as a pastor whenever he was not directly involved with his work at the factory. On evenings and weekends, he would visit some of our church members in the area, studying the Bible with them and encouraging them in the faith. On Sabbaths, he took charge of the Bible study and preaching service. Although freedom of religion was not officially restored by the government, we lived in a sheltered place away from the city and direct observation by the communists. Any pastoral work that my father did still had to be done discretely without attracting too much attention.

Because the conditions were so unstable under communist rule, we knew that eventually it would be dangerous for us if we settled in this location permanently. We secretly inquired what options were available to us. The East German border was close, which would make it easier for us to make our escape to freedom. My father also knew some people that lived a short distance from the German border whom he could trust and could provide us with information on the best place and time to cross. It would not be a simple matter to cross with our whole family without being detected. Crossing the border with one or two people would pose less risk than a family of six, but we did not want to break up our family again and risk being separated permanently. We felt that God had miraculously brought us together, and He could also keep us safe as we crossed the border as a complete family. We knew that we could trust my father's employer, though he really did not want us to leave him. He was wholly in agreement that we might not be safe in the long run if we did stay there.

As we reflected on the years of the war and all that we had experienced thus far, it was obvious to us that without the Lord's leading and protection, none of us would have survived, nor would we be reunited as a complete family. As we considered the many wonderful, even miraculous, answers to prayer for protection and guidance, our faith for the future increased and we could see clearly that God had a definite plan for our lives. That was the courage that we needed now as we prepared for our most dangerous act of escape to West Germany.

Some things you don't see clearly when going through a trying experience, but as you look back on those times, the picture suddenly becomes much clearer. This was our experience as we considered how we ended up so close to the East German border at the end of the war making it possible to even consider crossing the border to freedom. With the German army coming into Ukraine and a number of other Soviet countries early on in the war, we were saved from being immediately sent to concentration camps in the east or to Siberia. Then, during German occupation we had some protection, even though we had lost our home and had become refugees. When the Russians drove the Germans back for a time, we too ended up going further back, and finally ended up in Poland. There we settled in any empty houses that were left standing from the war. These were the homes of the Polish people that the Germans drove out. Now as the war came to an end, the Polish people came back to reclaim their homes, and so we were driven further west to East Germany. This is exactly where we needed to be if we were to stand the slightest chance of crossing the border into West Germany. Everything was perfectly coming into place, but there were still two major steps to take to complete our journey to freedom: escape to Germany and immigrate to Canada. Because we had endured so much under communist rule, my father did not feel completely safe until we had put an ocean between us and the war-torn countries of Europe.

The time had come for us to make our way as close to the border as possible without raising any suspicion with the authorities. We said good-bye to our dear friend at the factory and made our way to a friend who lived very near to the border. We were now close enough to cross over in one night. We had a season of special prayer invoking the Lord to send His protecting angels to accompany us on this very dangerous venture. We knew if the guards saw us, we would certainly be shot. Every possible precaution had to be taken, and we could leave nothing to chance. My father heard of a man who lived adjacent to the border, who acted as a guide taking people across the border for a fee. We did not have much money of course, but we would give it a try and ask him if he would be willing to be our guide. Immediately searching out this man, my father hopefully presented his request. Our intense excitement at the thought of being in a country of freedom within the next twenty-four hours did not last long. The guide explained that he would no longer take anyone across the border because just the previous night a group of people had ventured to cross and five had been shot. We were originally scheduled to be with that group. We were now so thankful that the Lord kept us from crossing the border that particular night. We later learned that the same night that we were to cross the border, a group attempted to cross and many were shot. What were we to do now?

In spite of the extreme danger of successfully crossing the border, my father was not willing to abandon our plans to do so. If the man was not willing to be our guide, we would select a Guide who had never failed us. We would totally trust the Lord to close the eyes of the border guards and lead us through the border, where we could worship Him in a country where freedom still existed. The decision was made to thoroughly question the guide giving us as much information as possible about when it would be advisable to cross if he was leading a group and what area of the border to cross. We knew that the Lord could protect us, but we had to do our part as well. The guide explained that the best time to cross was early in the morning before the night shift went off duty. By that time, they were tired and might not be as observant as when they first started their shift. He also warned us not to make any noise that might alert the guards. I remember my father having a talk with my brother and me. He told us that if we were to fall down during our crossing of the border and hurt ourselves, even if the blood was gushing, we were not to utter a sound, or it could cost us our lives. He made that point very clear, and we did not fail to understand the seriousness of his instruction.

If the man was not willing to be our guide, we would select a Guide who had never failed us. We would totally trust the Lord to close the eyes of the border guards and lead us through the border, where we could worship Him in a country where freedom still existed.

The guide further instructed us to go through the border in a particular place. He said, "Go early in the morning down a certain road, and presently you will come to a railroad track. When you see the marker that I told you about, you need to cross the tracks. Before you cross the tracks, take note of a wire that is on either side of the tracks. The wire is about eighteen inches off the ground and attached to metal stakes with porcelain insulators. If you touch the wire on either side, it will give off a zinging sound that will immediately alert the guards. Make sure that you step high over the wire without making contact, otherwise, your escape will come to a sudden end. After you have successfully crossed the tracks you will see a small, almost imperceptible path leading into a wooded area. Follow this path and it will lead you to a clearing. You will need to continue in the same direction until you come to a broken-down fence. On the other side of that fence is West German territory. This area has not been walked on too much, therefore, you will need to pay close attention not to change directions as you proceed. There are guards stationed about every kilometer apart. The guards may change the nature of their patrol at times, without notice. They could go from their post of duty to the place where the next guard is stationed and back again during each hour, in which case you would, at best, have thirty minutes to cross, if not detected. Two guards might also decide to meet each other in the middle of their stations and then return within the same hour. In that case, one would have fifteen minutes or less to try to make it to freedom, provided the timing is right as well. If you stray from the area that I recommend you take as you cross, you could easily meet up with the guards." We thanked him for his instructions and advice and resolved to be on our way early the next morning.

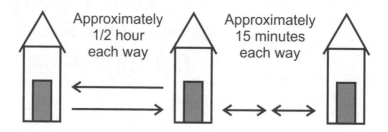

Early the next morning we asked the Lord to be with us and save us from the dangers ahead. We took only our most essential belongings and needed items for the trip and strapped them onto two bicycles that were still in our possession, enabling us to carry a lighter load. The bicycles basically served us as a wheelbarrow which we pushed along as we walked. Now we made our way down the road to where the railroad track was. It was still a little dark as the sun had not yet appeared. We anxiously followed the directions we were given and were delighted when the first sign of the railroad track appeared. We next looked for the place where we were to cross the tracks. The whole escape was expected to take only several hours, but tension was high for fear that we might miss following some of the crucial directions we had been given. We could not afford to make even the slightest mistake. Now we came to where we were to cross the tracks. We were extremely careful to lift both bicycles over the wires without making contact and sounding the alarm. In the darkness, the wires on both sides of the tracks were not easily visible. We were much relieved after we had successfully crossed the tracks and cleared the wire on both sides. We now found the path that the guide had told us about. The path was hard to follow since it was used infrequently, and we moved slowly forward without uttering a sound. Everyone was on full alert. Every movement we made was deliberate, and our minimal conversation was spoken in quiet, whispering tones. The path led us further into the wooded area, and if the suspense had not been so intense, it might have been a relaxing walk through the woods. Gradually, signs of the approaching morning light helped us to see our way more clearly, but we were also more vulnerable. Now the guards also had a clearer view of the surroundings they were patrolling.

Walking further into the wooded area, we remembered that we had been strongly advised by the guide to pay very careful attention to the path we were to follow. It was not a clearly marked path, and if we did not carefully examine each step, we could easily take a wrong turn that would lead us in the direction where the guards were patrolling. If we

We felt quite sure that we were still going in the right direction when, all of a sudden, we noticed the form of a man dressed in a uniform approaching us. Our hearts sank as we thought of what was about to take place. Had we come so far only to be sent back, or worse, lose our life? My father took the lead, and as the officer was now in clear view, he asked, "Are you escaping?" What could my father say? It was quite obvious what our intention was. Father's reply was, "Yes."

should meet up with them there would be no second chance. They would shoot first and ask questions later. We felt quite sure that we were still going in the right direction when, all of a sudden, we noticed the form of a man dressed in a uniform approaching us. Our hearts sank as we thought of what was about to take place. Had we come so far only to be sent back, or worse, lose our life? My father took the lead, and as the officer was now in clear view, he asked, "Are you escaping?" What could my father say? It was quite obvious what our intention was. Father's reply was, "Yes." "Not the way you are going," he said, "You are headed right in the direction of the patrolling guard. You must retrace your steps a certain distance, and you will again come to the path you evidently veered away from." Now that we were close to the officer, we noticed that he was not armed, and obviously we had not been shot. What a relief. We were still alive! Although he was in a uniform, it was not the uniform of a patrol guard, but of a forestry officer. He detected our fear of having been discovered when just shortly before we had been confident that we were still on the right course. He then gave us words of encouragement that helped rebuild our confidence. "Don't be afraid. You need to go back a bit and then you will again be on the right path. After that, follow the directions that you were given very carefully, and you will come to the fence which is the border to West Germany." We were so delighted and thanked him profusely for his kindness. We were now determined to be even more careful not to take the wrong turn again.

We corrected our mistake, and as we continued on our way through the wooded area, we wondered what had happened. How could we have veered off in the wrong direction when we were so careful to follow the instructions we had been given? Sometimes when going through a wooded area, it is possible to lose your sense of direction and you end up going in circles. Is that what happened to us? We noted that the directions the forestry officer gave us were identical to the ones we were originally given by the guide who was not willing to lead our family across the border. We now gathered new courage acutely aware that every detail must be strictly followed if we were to succeed. Success was life. Failure was almost certainly death.

With great care we continued on our way as quietly as possible so as not to attract attention to our whereabouts. The birds began to wake up and fill the air with their songs of praise, and in our hearts we joined them, praising God for His goodness and care. We had just experienced His certain leading when He sent the forestry officer at just the right time. If

He had not, we would have headed directly into the path of the patrolling guard.

Everything went quite well for the next hour or so. We were now more cautious than ever. We presently came to an area where it was almost impossible to figure out where the path continued. It seemed that the path had disappeared completely. What should we do? If only we could ask someone that was familiar with these woods. There was, however, no time for long delays. We had to make a decision and hope it was the right one. We had not gone very far when we again saw an officer approach us. Our hearts trembled with fear. Had we come so far only to be captured and sent back? As the officer approached us, we realized that he resembled the first one in that he was not armed. What a relief! Could we trust him? Even though he was an East German forestry officer, it was not unheard of that he might turn us in to the authorities to earn favor with the controlling communists. His question to us was like that of the first, "Are you trying to escape?" "Yes," my father replied. Sensing our great fear he said, "Don't be afraid. You are heading in the wrong direction right now, and if you keep going that way you will definitely meet up with the patrolling guard. You must make a quick correction, and then you will be on the right path again. You are getting much closer to your destination." *What a relief.* The Lord sent this man at just the right time.

> *Our escape to freedom was an experience that will stay with me for life. Our faith was tested to the limit, but we put our trust in God and He never failed us.*

Invigorated and with great anticipation we moved ahead, hoping to soon see the fence that we were told was the border to West Germany. Our escape to freedom was an experience that will stay with me for life. Our faith was tested to the limit, but we put our trust in God and He never failed us. What a wonderful God we serve. But now again, the unexpected happened. Could it be that we had lost our way again? Coming toward us was another forestry officer. It was unheard of for three forestry officers to control such a small area. He, like the other two, helped us to find the right path that we obviously had lost, and assured us that we could not possibly lose our way now since we were almost in sight of our goal. Those were very tense moments, but we had come too far to turn back and our determination to be free had not diminished. True to his word, we did not have to continue much further until we saw the fence. This was the border! There was West Germany! *There was freedom!*

After we crossed the border, we were ecstatic. This is an experience that must be personally felt in order to truly understand the overwhelming emotion of utter joy, relief and unspeakable thankfulness it emotes in the one that has gone through it, and grasp what it means to be free. We longed to relax and enjoy this moment of triumph, but we knew that we must not linger long so close to the border. If an East German guard saw us it was still possible that he could capture us and take us back or shoot us if he chose to do so. As we were thinking these thoughts we hastened to a road, now West German territory, when a fully armed soldier on a bicycle came in our direction. We at once feared that he was there to harm us. But this fear was short-lived. He whistled a tune as he passed by without paying much attention to any of us. We realized that this officer was a West German officer patrolling the border. He was actually there to keep us safe from the East German guards, but we did not realize it at that moment. Fear is a terrible thing that has the tendency to destroy trust. After living in a land for many years where fear was prevalent, it would take a while to build up trust again.

Thankfully, the border was now behind us, and we continued on for a few minutes until we felt safe enough to take a short time to recover from one of the most strenuous and exhausting trials we had ever experienced. Before us was an area of lush, green grass and thick moss that beckoned us to take a little rest from the stress of the frightful ordeal that was now behind us. We gratefully sat down beside a little stream of crystal-clear water that helped to revive and refresh us. There we also had a chance to thank our God for sparing our lives and protecting us from the many dangers we had encountered that day. We also thanked Him for protecting us from the dangers we were not aware of and may only realize when we are in that better land where sin and its effects will be forever banished. As we reflected on the happenings of the day, the question came to our mind, "Who were the three forestry officers that helped us stay the course, and make our escape possible?" We may never know the answer to that question this side of the kingdom.

Almost reluctantly, we left this lovely and peaceful scene and continued on to the nearest city, and then to the railway station. The West German government had arranged for all refugees like us to board a train from this area to take us to a larger center where accommodations were provided for those who had lost everything. Aboard the train, my father noticed quite a bit of excitement at the other end of our train car. There were ten young men in their early twenties having a very lively discussion so my father, being the people person that he was, made his way over to where they were and asked what all the excitement was about. "Oh," they replied, "there were about 100 of us who were determined to escape East Germany and to cross the border to West Germany. Last night we decided to storm the border, but unfortunately most of our group did not make it, but we are now free and fortunate to have come through alive." Two of them had been wounded in the process; one had been shot in the arm, and the other in the hand. They had used a handkerchief to bind up their wounds, but when concern was expressed over their injuries, their response was, "These wounds will heal, but we are now free." They had to pay a big price for freedom, and we well knew what that meant.

Soon the train arrived at its destination where we were to be given a place of shelter. Usually the housing consisted of hundreds of people settling temporarily in large auditoriums, empty factory warehouses or other facilities that offered little or no privacy. We, however, felt like kings. We were now in a land of freedom. Now there was one goal left for us to reach. We would now try to locate our relatives in Canada and start the immigration process.

Chapter 9

In Search of Liberty

Our safe arrival into West Germany and exposure to the freedoms that it offered was like a surreal dream. Crossing the border and coming through unscathed, while the outcome for thousands of others who had endeavored to escape and had suffered grim consequences, generated a heart of gratitude in each one of us. Though still refugees without a home, we were now in a country that accepted us and provided for our basic necessities.

As a result of the suffering we had endured under communist rule, my father feared that West Germany was too close to Russia for us to make this country our permanent place of residence. It was his ultimate goal to move his family to Canada. It was only as he put a far-off distance between us and Russia that he would feel thoroughly safe. The first thing he must now do was locate his mother and sister who had previously immigrated to Canada, advising them of our successful crossing over into West Germany. He then inquired at the Canadian Immigration Office to see what the requirements were for immigration to Canada. Here another challenge was placed before us. As refugees, the Russians had taken all of our passports and identification papers. It was now necessary to locate someone who had known us well for some time and could swear as to our identity.

When it comes to government institutions, the wheels churn slowly, and so it was with the immigration process. We soon realized that it would probably be several years before we could hope to board a ship to Canada—if we were cleared by immigration. As the process was explained to us, we first had to find someone in Canada who would be our sponsor and guarantee to be responsible for our family for one year. Then we must find an employer that would guarantee work for my father for one year. The place of work had to be on a farm at a minimum wage since farmers could not afford to pay high wages or find workers who would labor for such a low remuneration. Work on the farms was intensive, especially during harvest time, and the pay was thirty-five cents an hour. This requirement was for one year, after which one could seek work elsewhere at the prevailing rate of just over a dollar an hour. After finding individuals willing to be guarantors, we had to undergo a thorough health examination by Canadian doctors who worked with Canada Immigration. Only those with perfect health were granted permission to immigrate. After passing all these requirements, the only word every immigrant was keen to hear was that one word of affirmation, "Okay." This was the first word that we learned in our study of the English vocabulary.

My father immediately contacted his mother who now lived in Ontario, Canada. Jubilant over the news of our escape, she did not hesitate to be the guarantor for our family for our first year in Canada. She also knew of a farmer friend of hers who was willing to offer my father work for the first year. Receiving this welcome news, we then started the process of health examinations for each member of our family. We were advised that this process could possibly take several years, or it could be accomplished within a year. It would depend on the doctor and our state of health.

After passing all these requirements, the only word every immigrant was keen to hear was that one word of affirmation, "Okay." This was the first word that we learned in our study of the English vocabulary.

In the interim, the German government endeavored to find a place for us to live. This was not an easy task. Germany had undergone massive damage from the thousands of bombs that had fallen over its territory causing ruination throughout the country, destroying in some cases complete cities. Now with the influx of countless refugees, there were not enough homes or apartments to accommodate everyone. The situation was bleak, but they did the best they could under the circumstances.

Auditorium where we stayed with walls of blankets as room dividers

We were housed for a short time in a large auditorium with up to 100 other people. This space was divided by blankets hung from wires in both directions to give every family a space of about twelve feet square. Army blankets served as our four walls. Bunk beds were set up in this square which served as both our sleeping and living quarters. There was absolutely no privacy, and if one leaned against the blanket wall you would find yourself in your neighbor's apartment. Sitting up in the top bunk would also give you an exceptional view of all your neighbors and their activities. We had no need of television. A community kitchen supplied the basics for meals. Compared to what we had come through, we thought we were now living as kings. Early every morning everyone was strongly urged to take part in an exercise program outside in the brisk air in order to keep us healthy while living in these crowded conditions. Since physical activity was limited here, my father encouraged my sister, who was a fine seam-stress, to hold sewing classes for the ladies who wished to attend. Right from the beginning, this venture was a great success. The ladies, and even some men, greatly appreciated the instruction.

We were in this situation for a while, but during the course of our stay in West Germany, we were frequently moved to various places. One of the places where we were housed was a large, two-story paper factory warehouse. Rather than having walls of blankets, cardboard walls were erected to give each family a little square for their living space. We could no longer look into our neighbor's apartment, but we could certainly hear their conversations.

The two-story paper factory warehouse, where we stayed with other refugees. The rooms were divided with thick cardboard.

My father, as a pastor, was now able to continue his pastoral duties in West Germany where freedom of religion existed. Each morning he would read from the Bible for our family worship, but our neighbor on the other side of the thin cardboard wall was an atheist and did not appreciate what he heard. Eventually though, he complained less and maybe even a little conversion took place from all that he heard each day.

With so many people living in such congested quarters, there was always plenty of action and never a dull moment. When we left East Germany, the factory owner where my dad had worked, gave me a large chocolate bar which I saved because I thought it was too valuable to eat. One of my friends saw it and was most anxious to get his hands on it. He had a harmonica that really caught my eye, and we soon agreed on an even trade. I've always been convinced that I got the better end of the deal. I soon learned to play that instrument and enjoyed many years of good music. My friend, however, once devouring the chocolate, had nothing more to show for it.

As we were being moved around from one place to another, the requirements of immigration for refugees were always before us. There seemed to be a lot of doctor's appointments for check-ups and follow-ups. One doctor had us coming back to him over and over again for the same thing without ever giving us a final approval that we were okay. We soon discovered that many others were having the same problem with him. Apparently, this doctor benefitted financially from seeing the same patients over and over again. After an appeal was made to the immigration office, this problem was investigated and the doctor was fired. The newly appointed doctor was much easier to work with. Many now received their approvals and their final clearance. Had a different doctor been in this position, we might have received our clearance to travel to Canada much sooner. At one point, the immigration authorities decided to move all the refugees that had applied for immigration to an area that had been used by the army during the war. There were many rows of army apartment buildings, some of which had been bombed, but most were still intact. The refugees were grouped according to their nationalities or religion, and the country they had chosen to immigrate to. As we had Mennonite names, we were placed with the Mennonites.

Group of Mennonites waiting for immigration; our family was in this group.

During our long wait there for immigration clearance, it was decided that arrangements must be made to address the educational needs for the many refugee children. Several teachers were found for the lower grades of the Mennonite school, but no one for the upper grades and the position of principal. My father was well-qualified for the position, but we were no longer a part of the Mennonite faith, therefore, they were reluctant to ask him to take this position. After a time when no one else was found for the position, they approached him and he accepted, and did a fine job. A little later, the pastor of the Mennonite church received his clearance from immigration and moved on. We were Seventh-day Adventists, but since my parents had grown up in the Mennonite faith, and my dad was a pastor, the elders of the church asked my dad to preach for them every Sunday morning. They stipulated, however, that they would appoint one of the elders to make sure that he preached on topics they would approve of. It was interesting indeed to have Dad preach on Sabbath in our church and on Sunday in the Mennonite church.

Teachers at the Mennonite school; Dad was the principal (middle, back row).

Dad and his students; my brother Arthur is 2ⁿᵈ from left—back row.

Immigration approval took much longer than we anticipated, but my dad was never idle. He kept very busy with his duties as a pastor, teacher and many other tasks during our waiting time. He studied the Bible with those who showed an interest, and he even organized a little church in a nearby town. At times we wondered if our approval to immigrate to Canada would ever come. It was more difficult to receive approval to immigrate to Canada or the United States than some of the countries in South America. At one point, we even considered immigrating to Paraguay or Uruguay since it was much easier to be granted entry there, but our family was in Canada, so that remained our first choice.

During this time, I explored the world around me. I was now in a country of more freedom than I had experienced all the previous years of my life. One thing that I noticed was the milkman who delivered milk to the houses in our area. He had several big cans in the back of his van full of milk. Every so often he would stop, open the back doors of his van, and the women who had gathered where he had come to a halt, would approach the van with their containers for milk. He would take his pitcher and fill all the containers the ladies brought him. They then paid him for the milk and he would drive to another area and repeat the same process. As I watched this exchange from one day to the next, I wished I could get a ride on this milk van. I had never had the privilege of riding in a vehicle like this before, and I felt that I was missing out on something special. In my mind I formulated a plan. I decided that the next day when the milkman made his deliveries, I would grab onto the back of the van and catch a ride. Well, things happened a little differently than I expected. After the milkman finished his deliveries and got back in his van, I grabbed hold of the back and hung on, exulting in this long-anticipated ride. I was having a wonderful time when, to my dismay, I realized that he was traveling farther and farther away from my home, and now I feared that I would not find my way back again. In my distress I did something very foolish. I let go of my hold, dropping to the hard surface of the cobblestone road. The result was disastrous. I broke my right collar bone, and the pain was unbearable. It was even worse after the doctor made a big ball of cast material, put it on my back, and strapped my body tightly to it so that my shoulder would heal in the proper position. I could not lie down at all for several weeks. I had to be in a sitting position day and night until my bones had healed. My parents, of course, were very upset with me, and they feared that my injuries might delay our departure to Canada. I did learn my hard-earned lesson, however, and never tried that again.

I wished I could get a ride on this milk van. I had never had the privilege of riding in a vehicle like this before, and I felt that I was missing out on something special. In my mind I formulated a plan. I decided that the next day when the milkman made his deliveries, I would grab onto the back of the van and catch a ride.

We made more trips to the immigration doctors and experienced yet more delays. Then, finally, my sister and my aunt (Mother's sister), received their final clearance. Now we had to decide what we should do. We were finally together as a united family; should we now split up again? What if our immigration clearance did not come through? Since we didn't have any reason to think that our clearance would not come through in a number of months, the decision was made to let them travel abroad right away, and the rest of us would follow as soon as we received our approval. I believe God impressed us that our decision was the best one under the circumstances. I now know that our plan was good as a delay on our part might have sent the wrong message to the immigration authorities. We said our emotional goodbyes to my sister and aunt as they boarded the ocean liner, *Skythia*, that would take them across the Atlantic to Canada. We at least knew that they were in good hands and were traveling to a country where they would be safe and free from communism.

My sister and my aunt, Anna Schulz, leaving by train to the ship port ready to travel to Canada. (left to right) Jacob, Arthur, Erna, Aunty (far right) Dad and Mom.

As we continued to wait for our approval to travel, we received some very discouraging news from my grandmother in Canada. Her letter explained that the farmer who had guaranteed work for my dad during our first year in Canada had retired and sold his farm. He could, therefore, no longer be our sponsor. He had forgotten that he had signed the papers to be our sponsor and was now very concerned what the Department of Immigration would do to him. Now we were worried too. Would we have to start all over again with the immigration process? Our family made this a special point of prayer, and Dad sent a letter to his mother with a message to his work sponsor telling him, "Do not worry. I will abide by the law and work for any farmers that need help for the minimum wages as specified, and no harm will come to you." The sponsor was much relieved for Dad's answer, and we were so thankful that we did not have to start all over again with paperwork.

One day, around this time, I was playing with a friend of mine who had two cute rabbits in a pen behind his house, and he asked me to come with him to give them some food. Another friend of his wanted to help him feed the rabbits and was jealous because I had been asked first. As the two of us were bent over the pen concentrating on the rabbits, he suddenly came up behind me and pushed me into the rabbit pen with such force that my head was thrust into the roof of the pen, which was a sheet of sharp tin. It all happened so fast that at first I didn't realize that I had been hurt. As I picked myself up from the fall, I saw that blood was dripping from my head. Putting my hand on the top of my head to investigate my injuries, I saw that there was blood everywhere. In a panic I ran to our house screaming. My parents immediately whisked me off to the doctor's office. The cut to the top of my head was about six inches long and so deep that the bone was exposed. The doctor soon had me cleaned and stitched up. When he had finished, my entire head was wrapped up as though I was wearing a turban. On returning home, the boy who had caused the injury was waiting at our house with his mother, apologizing profusely for what he had done. Everything was soon forgiven, and I was prepared to move on. My parents, however, were

> *The day finally arrived. It was May 18, 1949, when we heard the long anticipated, best and only word of the English language that we had learned: the word "Okay."*

deeply concerned that we might now be held back from boarding the ship to Canada until my injuries were completely healed. I am glad to say that the bandages were able to come off just before our scheduled departure date, for which my parents were greatly relieved.

The day finally arrived. It was May 18, 1949, when we heard the long anticipated, best and only word of the English language that we had learned: the word "Okay." We had received our final clearance to board the ocean liner, *Samaria*. With great excitement and rejoicing, we prepared for this long-awaited event now only a few days away. The time had finally come for us to board the ship that would take us across the Atlantic to our new home. How we looked forward to arriving at our final destination and the fulfillment of our plans to resettle in a land of freedom!

What a grand experience this was for me. I had never been on such a large ship. The trip took twelve days where we saw nothing but sky and ocean. The food was especially delicious. We were served oranges and other fruit that we could only dream of when we were in Russian-controlled countries. There is sometimes a downside to sea travel, however, and after a few days on the ocean, more than half of the passengers were seasick. I don't want to describe how this affected the people that contracted the sickness, only to say that it is a very nauseous, debilitating condition. My dad and I were the only fortunate ones from our family who did not get sick.

After nearly two weeks, we saw in the far distance the first signs of land. This was Canada, our new country of freedom that we had planned and longed over for so many years. It was like a dream come true when we finally pulled into the Quebec City Harbor. We were elated when our feet first touched the soil of our newly adopted country. Gathering up our belongings, we boarded a train and rode for several hours to a little town in Ontario called Baden. Here my cousin awaited our arrival in his Model T Ford. This was my first car ride in Canada and the first ride where I could sit inside the car, rather than hanging onto the back.

We had a joyous and memorable reunion with our family. Just imagine the glad hearts of my dad and his mother who had not seen each other for almost twenty-five years. Sadly, we would not have a long time with her, but we were able to be together for nearly one year in her humble, little home before she passed to her rest.

Our long journey had finally come to an end. Oh, the price of freedom! Do we really always value it as we should?

Chapter 10

Continual Guidance and Care

The sounds of battle from that war have long been silenced. Those years of violent aggression that engaged the entire world in its hostilities are now in the past. God's loving care for His children then, now and forever, however, has not and will not change. We may not be aware of the times that He has intervened in our lives to keep us from harm or directed us in making right decisions, or acknowledge His care for us imagining that we were wise enough to avoid a disaster. There are several instances in my life where God's protection and care were evident in my travels overseas and even here at home in Canada. Some of these experiences I will share in this closing chapter.

The years have quickly passed, and it seems as though there was never enough time to fit everything in that I would have liked to become part of my life and who I am. Life is lived in a different way when living in a free country. Now that fear no longer overshadowed each day, I could now concentrate on living a fuller and more enjoyable life. There were always the occasional ups and downs and possible roadblocks to be dealt with but, in general, there was at last a wonderful feeling of security.

The first challenge I faced when we came to Canada was to learn a new language. We had arrived just before the beginning of the school summer holiday. On my first day at school I was prepared to be placed in the fourth grade, and to be promoted to the fifth grade in the fall. I had a slight problem, however, as I could neither understand, nor read or write English. After assessing the situation, the teacher told me, through a student interpreter who translated her words to me in German, to enjoy a few extra weeks of summer holiday and return in September to start the full year. At first disappointed, I later realized that she had a purpose in her plan. I now had the whole summer to spend with my Canadian friends, and being young, I picked up quite a bit of the English language during the summer from my playmates. By the time September came along I could at least communicate with my teacher in English. As embarrassed as I was to start in first grade instead of fifth grade, I was assured that I could skip grades once my English grammar and spelling had improved. Within a couple of years, I was back on track and in the grade I was supposed to be in for my age. Learning a new language was a challenge, but with the encouragement of my teacher and fellow students, it was not long before I felt quite comfortable speaking this new tongue. It was much more difficult for my parents, unfortunately, and I had to be an interpreter for them on many occasions.

Our family was essentially destitute when we arrived in Canada. My father had to work long and hard hours to repay our fare on the ship from Germany to Canada. As a family, we all had to pitch in as we worked to establish ourselves in a new land. After completing the lower grades, most of my high school education was achieved by correspondence while I worked at odd jobs to help with the family finances. Later, I decided to try my skills at a farming business. It was always my desire to train for the ministry, but since it would involve at least seven years of college and university training, I felt it would not be possible to raise the funds necessary to finance this type of education. I resolved to stay with the farming business until something else might develop. After a few rough years of learning the trade, my financial picture changed substantially. I then began to consider that if I could sell my farming operation for its anticipated value, I might possibly see my way through the seven years of college and university necessary to train as a minister. It was my plan at that time to combine business and ministry, and to eventually enter into an administrative position. This was the seemingly impossible dream that I wanted to strive for. My father always instilled in his children to set high goals and to get as much education as possible.

None of this would be possible, of course, unless I was able to sell my business for the price needed to finance my lofty plans. I would also need to sell my farming operation without securing the services of a real estate agent so that I would not have a hefty commission to pay to the agent. I had to ensure that I would have sufficient funds for food, lodging and tuition for the seven years of education that I needed to complete. I prayed, asking God to help me achieve my goal if it was in His plan for me to do so.

Having made my decision to sell the farming business under these conditions, I then made it known to everyone I came in contact with that my business was for sale. I did not have long to wait. Friday was one of my busiest times of the week because this was the day that I prepared for the Sabbath. Since I would do no regular work on that day, except what was absolutely necessary, I made sure that all arrangements for the Sabbath were taken care of before sundown and the beginning of the Sabbath. I had learned this valuable lesson from my parents while we were refugees in Europe. If we were able to keep the Sabbath during those difficult years under communism, there was certainly no reason why we couldn't do it now in this country of freedom.

The afternoon was busy as I took care of the last of the chores. Unexpectedly, there was a knock on the door. There stood three men who explained that they had come to inquire if our business was still for sale, and to ask about the terms and conditions of making the purchase. I assured them that it was still for sale, but that I would not have much time to show them everything that day. I encouraged them to come back on Monday when I would have more time to go over all the details with them. They persisted, however, asking if I could at least give them a whirl-wind tour of everything, and then they would come back the next Monday to finalize on the details of the purchase. I had just enough time for what they requested and agreed to do so. Was I excited? Of course, I was. Since the sun was soon to set, however, I felt it was more important for me to obey my God than to sell my business. According to the commandment, He has asked us to put all work aside on His holy day, and to spend it with Him in worship and praise. I had just enough time to show them the two large buildings and the house. They said they liked what they saw and agreed with the price, but they did not want to leave without giving me a substantial amount of money as a down payment. They wanted to return the following Monday to take care of the details and the rest of the paperwork. Showing my surprise at their response and their eagerness to make the purchase, they explained that they had looked at a similar farming operation the week before, and when they came to purchase it, it was already sold. They wanted to be sure that I would not sell it to anyone else. We agreed, they went on their way and our family kept the Sabbath. On Monday they were back, and we finished the deal.

Now God had made it possible, by providing the funds, for me to finish my training. This was truly a miracle. With the assurance that I had God's blessing, I enrolled in college and began my seven-year training program. The road ahead would not always be easy, but God never failed me. Each answer to prayer gave me the strength to meet the next looming challenge that I faced.

It was while I was taking my first college class that I experienced the next answer to prayer. The college that I attended was about a five-hour drive from where our business had been. After moving my family to this new area, I enrolled and registered for classes. The long list of textbooks that I needed for my first quarter caused me to wonder how I could possibly read that many books in ten weeks and remember everything that they contained. Regardless, I resolved to do my best and moved forward. Admittedly, on occasion I wondered if I had made the right decision in selling our beautiful place in the country with its comfortable income, for seven years of uncertainty at school. With having been out of school and in the workplace for a number of years, I found that school was not always easy for me. My first class was history which required a lot of memorization of dates and events. I had to do an enormous amount of reading to prepare for each class, and then prepare for three two-hour exams during the first quarter. Well I studied and studied and studied some more until I thought my head would explode with all the facts and figures. I read hundreds of pages and when I closed the textbook, I was devastated when I realized that I couldn't remember a single thing I had read. Again and again I reread the same chapters, but I couldn't seem to concentrate on what I had just read. Perhaps it was because I had been out of school for so many years, and my mind had not adjusted to focusing on academics. The evening before the first major exam was scheduled I studied till late in the evening, and the next morning I was back at it by 4 a.m. I was now so stressed that I was mixing up dates and facts, and the exam was only an hour away. Of one thing I was certain; I had done my best and could not have studied any harder. I also knew I had to pass this exam in order to continue with my education. As the saying goes, I had burned all my bridges behind me, and the only thing to do was to move forward with my plan. Before leaving the house, I knelt down to pray and asked the Lord to see me through this most difficult time, and then I was on my way.

As the class sat there waiting, the professor handed out the exam papers and then offered a prayer for the class, asking God to give us a clear mind so we would do our very best. "Of course," he said, "that only applies to those of you who studied. If you did not do your part, the Lord can't reward you." Well, I knew I had studied like I had never studied before. Tentatively, I looked at the exam and read the first question. The answer came in a flash. It was the same for the second, the third and right through the 100 questions that were on the exam. Every answer came to me as soon as I had finished reading each question. I ended up at the top of the class of about 100 students. This experience was very humbling. I had no doubt that it was an answer to my prayer that brought me such positive results. This was just the encouragement that I needed. Now I could face anything. God will always come through for us if we put Him first in everything we do.

> *Tentatively, I looked at the exam and read the first question. The answer came in a flash. It was the same for the second, the third and right through the 100 questions that were on the exam.*

There were many other classes and challenges ahead, but my courage was strong because I had experienced God's blessings when I needed it most. With so many classes and all the reading and reports that went with it, I needed to refresh my mind occasionally. So, whenever time would permit and we had an extra-long weekend, our family would take a five-hour trip to visit my dad and my sister and her family in Ontario, Canada. This gave me a welcome relief from the heavy study program, and our children had a chance to spend time with my sister and her family of seven, as well as Grandpa. My mother was no longer alive, so Grandpa got all the attention. On these trips, which happened about four times a year, I would usually take a lot of textbooks with me, but most of the time I didn't open a book. I learned that taking a needed break free from studies was revitalizing, and when we came back from our trip, my grades did not suffer.

It was during one of these trips that our family again experienced a remarkable intervention from our merciful Father. After selling our business in Ontario, and before I settled into years of studies, we purchased a brand-new Buick that we thought would serve us well until graduation. This car was now just a few months old and was very comfortable, as well as reliable. We were very excited to visit with our family in Ontario, and after loading the car with everything we thought we needed, plus a few things that could have been left behind, we were off.

Most of this trip was on a major four-lane divided highway in Michigan, which bypassed all the cities along the way. There was always something special to talk about as we traveled along since my studies were not occupying my mind while I was on vacation. All went well for a few hours, and then I noticed that our new car was losing speed. The speed limit on this highway was seventy miles an hour, with the slowest speed permitted at forty-five miles per hour. Our car's speed went from seventy ... to sixty ... to fifty no matter how hard I pushed down on the accelerator. Only emergency stops were permitted on this highway, and it was becoming obvious that an emergency that I was powerless to stop was developing. As the car's speed fell to thirty miles per hour on this busy highway, I had no choice but to pull off to the side of the road as far as I could to avoid being the cause of an accident. We sat there while the traffic whizzed past us. The motor was still running, but the car had no power. I could make no sense of what was happening. I had taken the car in for its regularly scheduled service inspection just prior to starting out on this trip and the car was found to be mechanically sound. Not knowing what else to do, I shut off the motor and sat there wondering what to do next. I looked at my watch and noted the time. We waited in the car for a few more minutes, which seemed like an interminable amount of time under these conditions, before I got out of the vehicle and opened the hood to see if there was something obvious that would explain our dilemma. Everything seemed to be in order, so I got back behind the wheel,

> *We at once realized that our car problem had delayed us for exactly ten minutes, and if we had not been delayed, we would have undoubtedly been involved in that pileup.*

turned the ignition and the car started without the slightest hesitation. I put it in gear and pressed down on the gas. In no time at all we were traveling fifty, sixty and then seventy miles an hour with no sign of any problems.

We were greatly relieved that we were back on the road, but completely baffled as to what had just happened. We traveled on for another mile or two when I saw several police cars up ahead stopping all traffic and routing all vehicles off the highway we were on, directing them onto a lengthy detour. As we approached the police officers, I questioned one of them as to the reason for the detour. He responded quickly saying, "Just about ten minutes ago we experienced a serious multiple car and truck pileup just ahead, and it will take hours before the highway will again be open for traffic."

We at once realized that our car problem had delayed us for exactly ten minutes, and if we had not been delayed, we would have undoubtedly been involved in that pileup. We were filled with wonder that our heavenly Father had placed His hand of protection and care over our family in such a way that averted what could have been a great disaster for us all. There were no further instances with our car the rest of our journey, and ever after as long as we owned that car. When we reached our destination, I stopped at a service center and had our car checked thoroughly, but the report from the service department was, "There is absolutely nothing wrong with your car." What a great God we serve!

Judy and Jacob Hiebert in the Middle East

There was another time when God worked in a miraculous way to save my life, or possibly the lives of both my wife Judy and myself. It was a very strange experience that I may not have the answer for until my guardian angel reveals it to me in God's kingdom. This was an instance where I experienced God's intervention from a possibly dangerous situation that I was not even aware of. My wife Judy and I were asked to travel to one of the Middle East countries where terrorism was not uncommon, and the government was not in control of all that was happening. We agreed to take on this assignment before I fully understood how unsafe and unstable an environment we were entering into, otherwise we probably would not have ventured to serve there.

A friend of ours whom we had previously worked with overseas asked us to come to this country where he was in charge of a humanitarian organization that provided aid that brought relief to those who found themselves in very desperate and pitiful situations. This would also involve working in several refugee camps. Since I was well acquainted with life as a refugee, I felt drawn to answer the call to serve and help make a difference where human suffering was at an all-time high. My wife and I were adept in treasury and administrative work, and we had just retired from active service a year earlier when the call of service came to us. Judy was asked to train the secretarial staff in the head office, and my assignment was to train the treasury staff. The work also involved doing an audit for a similar Canadian organization that was connected with this office. It sounded challenging, but we felt that we were prepared for the task. We made our arrangements for the trip and were soon on our way. Our assignment was for a three-month period, and we were to work as volunteers.

Since we were advised that it would not be a good idea for us to operate a vehicle in that country, arrangements were made to have a driver from the office pick us up from our residence and bring us back again at the end of the day. Housing was provided and food was available, though usually not the kind we were used to or acquainted with. But we did not go hungry. Since we were vegetarians, most of our groceries came from small fruit and vegetable stands along the roadside where young boys were in charge, and who were overjoyed when we purchased our produce from them. There were no supermarkets as we know them. For those who depended on meat as their basic diet, they found all meat products to be very fresh and very much alive. Cattle, sheep, goats and poultry were kept in pens downtown along the main street of this good-sized city. People would make their selection, and purchase the animal which was then butchered there before their eyes, enabling them to go home with very fresh meat. This process was necessary because of the hot climate in this country, and most people did not have any refrigeration in their homes. We were surrounded by poverty and we witnessed many diseases that reminded us of the time when Jesus was on earth. Many of these unfortunate people were born blind or deaf, and many were deformed or paralyzed. Women were completely covered in black apparel and only their eyes were visible. Two young girls worked as secretaries in the office and assisted me with some of the work I was responsible for. Clothed as they were, I could not tell them apart until I realized that one wore glasses and the other did not.

Some of the common people I worked with were very appreciative of what we did for them. However, as a whole, foreigners were treated with distrust. The state religion of Islam did nothing to help the situation. Wherever we went we were aware that many eyes were watching our every move. There were three large mosques near our residence and on several occasions, as the worshippers came from their religious activities, thousands of eyes were checking us out with disapproving stares. We tried as much as possible to avoid eye contact, but it still made us feel somewhat uneasy.

Almost immediately after arriving in this part of the world I developed pain in my right leg and hip. At first, I tried to dismiss it thinking it would pass in a few days, but instead of getting better it grew steadily worse until I found walking difficult. It was with severe pain and great effort that I climbed the stairs to our house and office. There seemed to be no explanation for why I was suddenly experiencing such pain. Prior to our arrival to this country, I had no hint of pain or of any potential problem that might cause such acute discomfort. There was a large German hospital in this city and since I had become acquainted with a German doctor, I made an appointment in the hope of getting some relief. After a thorough examination, the doctor could find no reason for my symptoms. He sent me to the hospital for X-rays and I waited patiently for the results, but they too showed nothing wrong with me. The pain in my leg and hip increased, and I was in sheer misery most of the time. Even the strongest pain medication did not provide any relief. I now longed to be back home in Canada where I was confident that I would be properly diagnosed and provided a cure for my ailment. We had, however, come to this country to serve the people who were depending on our help, and we determined to stay until our mission was completed.

I recall that one day when I was not at the office and we were in need of some vegetables to prepare a meal, Judy and I decided to go to the nearest roadside stand to make a few purchases. The pain in my leg and hip was at its worst this day, and I could only walk three or four steps at a time before resting a bit. We repeated this slow process until we had completed our walk. It was only about two blocks to the stand, but in my extreme discomfort it seemed as if it were several miles. I did not trust to send Judy out on her own because I was unsure of her safety. This was a country where men were dominant over the subservient women who were not always treated with their due respect. We opted to walk together, and it took us more than half an hour to cover this short distance. On our way back home with our purchases, we passed a large mosque where hundreds of worshippers happened to be leaving the building. We were aware that we were now a spectacle with all eyes upon us. Helplessly, I took a few steps then had to stop and hold on to Judy, repeating the process over and over until we finally arrived home. It was an extremely embarrassing experience for me. Fortunately, the day of our return to Canada was drawing closer, and we felt relieved that the end was now in sight.

Having completed our mission, we made our final travel plans as our departure date approached. Due to my severe pain and slow progress in walking, Judy ordered a wheelchair for our arrival at the Chicago O'Hare Airport. As often happens, our trip turned out to be quite different than we had expected. Our tickets were for a direct flight to Chicago, but instead our plane touched down in Jordan. We were advised that we had to spend the night there and continue on the next morning. Meals and accommodation were provided at a hotel close to the airport. On checking, we were told there were no planes available that day to take us on our journey overseas. We weren't given a good reason for the delay, but one of the local passengers informed us that this was one of the holiest days of the year for Muslims and all planes were needed to take the worshippers on their Hajj to Mecca.

The next morning, we were up early in anticipation of continuing our flight to Chicago. The plane took off on schedule, and while in the air I selected the map that traced our air travel on the screen in front of me. We were several thousand feet in the air when we noticed that the plane was turning more than usual. I assumed that it must be a usual flight pattern, and that once the captain was on course the plane would fly in a straighter line. Keeping my eyes on the screen, however, I could see that we continued to go in circles. A few minutes passed, and then the captain announced that we were experiencing computer problems and that there were indications that the landing gear might not be functioning properly. Reassuring us that we were not in danger, he further announced that we were returning to the Jordan airport to have the problem checked out. We continued to circle around for another half hour, and as it flew in this pattern, we noticed that the plane was dumping its fuel. Now we knew that all was not well, and several passengers tearfully made calls to their loved ones not expecting to survive this traumatic experience. As we approached the runway in preparation for landing, we saw that the runway was lined with emergency vehicles, fire trucks and police cars ready to leap into action if the landing gear did not engage.

In the midst of all this activity we realized the magnitude of the danger we were in. Though we felt concern as to what was happening around us, we experienced a quiet calmness because we knew Someone greater was in charge of our welfare. We knew that without God's loving care and protection we were not safe anywhere at any time. The landing gear did engage as the plane approached the runway, and we were thankful that we landed safely. On landing, we asked the captain his opinion of the events that we had just undergone. He confirmed that we had been in great danger of a crash landing, and the reason for all the emergency vehicles and the fire trucks was to help with the possible evacuation of the passengers, and the possibility of the plane catching on fire. The problem did indeed turn out to be a computer problem which was corrected, and after a further four-hour delay we were back in the air with the same plane. Our continued flight to Chicago and on to Canada was without further incident.

While at the airport in Jordan I noticed some relief of the pain in my leg and hip, and I was able to walk with a little less difficulty. By the time we reached the Chicago airport, I had no more pain and had no need of the wheelchair Judy had ordered for me. What a marvelous relief to be free from the acute, incessant pain that I had gone through for almost three months. The pain was finally gone, but the baffling question remained: how was it that I was suddenly healed?

The only way we can explain it is that we were in danger of being physically harmed while we were overseas. The people where we were, however, had compassion for the elderly and people with disabilities. I did not think of myself as being elderly even though I was retired, but I expect I was indeed a spectacle while struggling to walk a painful step or two before I needed support from my petite wife. Perhaps God allowed me to go through this experience so that the people did not see me as a threat to them, but someone worthy of compassion. Though not today, someday I will know why I had to go through this painful experience. It has been twelve years since this happened to me and I have had no more pain in my leg or hip and had no need for treatments. I am so thankful for the care of my heavenly Father, even when I am not aware that I am in danger. May all of us take note of the many times God has intervened on our behalf and stop to thank Him for His loving care and safekeeping.

As I reflect over the many hardships and struggles in life that we have experienced as a family, the anxious times when life was uncertain from one day to the next, I am longing for the ultimate freedom in a world where all the effects of sin are gone forever. I long to live where freedom exists such as we have not known in this world. Jesus invites us to share that with Him when He says, *"Let not your heart be troubled: ye believe in God, believe also in me. In my Father's house are many mansions: if it were not so, I would have told you. I go to prepare a place for you. And if I go and prepare a place for you, I will come again, and receive you unto myself; that where I am, there ye may be also"* (John 14:1–3).

> *I am so thankful for the care of my heavenly Father, even when I am not aware that I am in danger. May all of us take note of the many times God has intervened on our behalf and stop to thank Him for His loving care and safekeeping.*

As long as we are in this world, we are still refugees seeking a better land where true freedom reigns. That is my final destination.

Bibliography

Geiermann, Peter. *The Convert's Catechism of Catholic Doctrine.* St. Louis, MO: B. Herder Book Co, 1957.

White, Ellen G. *Education.* Mountain View, CA: Pacific Press Publishing Association, 1903.

White, Ellen G. *The Great Controversy.* Mountain View, CA: Pacific Press Publishing Association, 1911.